MORE IDEAS

FOR

SCIENCE PROJECTS

MORE
IDEAS
FOR
SCIENCE
PROJECTS

ROBERT GARDNER

AN EXPERIMENTAL
SCIENCE SERIES BOOK

FRANKLIN WATTS
NEW YORK/LONDON
TORONTO/SYDNEY/1989

Illustrations by Vantage Art

Library of Congress Cataloging-in-Publication Data
Gardner, Robert, 1929-
More ideas for science projects/by Robert Gardner.
    p.   cm.—(An Experimental science series book)
Bibliography: p.
Includes index.
Summary: Presents ideas for an exploration of how to set up
science projects in the areas of astronomy, ecology, energy,
biology, anatomy, botany, physics, and engineering.
ISBN 0-531-10676-4
1. Science projects—Juvenile literature. [1. Science projects.]
I. Title. II. Series.
Q182.3.G37   1989
507'.8—dc19   88-39244   CIP   AC

CONTENTS

Other Books by Robert Gardner

Energy Projects for Young Scientists

Ideas for Science Projects

Kitchen Chemistry

Save That Energy

Science and Sports

Science Around the House

Science Experiments

The Whale Watchers' Guide

The Young Athlete's Manual

Water: The Life-Sustaining Resource

INTRODUCTION

This book will help you learn more about the methods of science by getting you involved in scientific investigations. Once you start trying to explain the natural world by designing and conducting experiments to answer questions, test the consequences of hypotheses, and check your predictions, you'll come to understand what the scientific method is all about. In fact, by rolling up your sleeves and probing nature directly, you'll understand the process of science far better than you ever will by reading about it in a textbook.

Some of the projects described here are designed for beginners just starting to carry out scientific investigations on their own. Others challenge readers who have conducted many experiments and have entered a number of science fairs. And a few of the projects, if successfully completed, would gain the investigator the respect of the entire scientific community. Such difficult projects are marked with an asterisk (*).

If you have not done a science project before, start with one that offers you guidance on how to do it.

Choose a topic that's interesting to you. If you have no special interest, choose something that requires materials that are readily available and get started. Once you're involved in the research, you'll find your interest growing as the pieces of the "puzzle" begin to fit together or raise new questions. Later, after you have done some experimentation, you'll probably want to work on projects that are more open-ended and that leave most of the details for you to figure out for yourself.

Don't try to make your results conform to a "right answer." Report your observations as you measured and sensed them. Be sure to include any possible sources of error and the ranges of these errors. Use a notebook or graph paper to record observations, make notes, plot graphs, design experiments and equipment, and write down conclusions and thoughts of your own and others that are related to your project.

It's a good idea to map out a procedure before you start your experimental work, but don't be surprised if you find that you want to change your approach halfway through your proposed plan. Despite what you may read in textbooks, the process of doing science is not a cut-and-dried procedure. While scientists generally do collect a reasonable amount of data before attempting to develop hypotheses or theories, their plans often change as they work, because science is filled with surprises. It's the surprises and unexpected turns of events that make science so interesting and exciting for those who seek to unravel nature's many mysteries.

Sometimes a project requires a control experiment. The control is used to be sure that only one factor at a time is being tested. For example, if you wanted to find out whether light has any effect on the germination of seeds, you would try to germinate two sets of seeds of the same plant. One set would be placed in light, the other set in darkness. All other conditions, such as temperature, moisture, air, and soil, would be the same so that you could be sure that the only difference between the seeds is whether or not they receive light.

If you found that the seeds germinated faster in light than in darkness, you might then try to find out if it is one particular color in the white light that causes the seeds to germinate faster. You would then have to germinate several sets of seeds under identical conditions except for the color of the light falling on them.

If you decide to enter your project in a science fair, you should plan to write a detailed report that includes the problem you investigated, the method you used, the results you obtained, and the conclusions that you drew based on the data collected. You would also include a bibliography of books or articles used in your research and an acknowledgment of those who helped you in any way. Charts, drawings, photographs, and graphs are useful in presenting your data to judges in an interesting and attractive way. Such a presentation may also be a good way to indicate the magnitude of the experimental errors that affect all experiments.

Whatever investigations you decide to do, do them safely, keeping in mind the rules listed below.

SAFETY FIRST

1. Do any experiments, whether from this book or of your own design, under the supervision of a science teacher or other knowledgeable adult, unless that person has approved your working by yourself.
2. Read all instructions carefully before proceeding with a project. If you have questions, check

with your supervisor before going any further.

3. Maintain a serious attitude while conducting experiments. Fooling around can be dangerous to you and to others.

4. Wear protective goggles when you are experimenting or are in a laboratory setting. Wear a lab apron if you are working with chemicals.

5. Do not eat or drink while experimenting and do not taste dry chemicals or solutions.

6. Do not inhale fumes released in a chemical reaction. Experiments involving poisonous or irritating gases should be done in a fume hood.

7. Keep flammable materials away from sources of heat.

8. Have safety equipment such as fire extinguishers, fire blankets, and first aid kits nearby while you are experimenting and know where this equipment is.

9. Keep your work area clean and organized. Don't mix experiments.

10. Turn off gas and electricity when they are not being used.

11. Clean up chemical spills immediately. If you spill something on your skin or clothing, rinse it off immediately with plenty of water and report what happened to a responsible adult.

12. Don't touch glass that has recently been heated; it looks the same as cool glass. Bathe skin burns in cold water or apply ice.

13. Do not touch any high-voltage source or anything connected to a high-voltage source.

14. Never experiment with household electricity without the supervision of a knowledgeable adult.

UNITS AND
THEIR ABBREVIATIONS
USED IN THIS BOOK

Length
mile (mi)
yard (yd)
foot (ft)
inch (in)
kilometer (km)
meter (m)
centimeter (cm)
millimeter (mm)

Area
square centimeter
(cm^2)

Volume
ounce (oz)
liter (L)
milliliter (mL)

Concentration
molar (M)

Mass
gram (g)

Power
watt (W)

Energy
calorie (cal)
joule (J)

Electrical units
volt (V)
ampere (A)
ohm (Ω)

Temperature
degrees Celsius (°C)
degrees Fahrenheit
(°F)

Time
hour (h)
minute (min)
second (s)

Frequency
hertz (Hz)

1
ASTRONOMY, LIGHT, AND SPACE

Do you enjoy looking at the stars and planets that dot the night sky? Do you find light and its interaction with matter interesting? Are you fascinated by the vast distances between the stars that you can see and between those stars and those of us who observe them? Do you think there may be other intelligent life forms in the universe trying to make contact with humans?

If your answer to any of these questions is yes, the projects in this chapter will probably be a good place to start.

ASTROPHOTOGRAPHY

Though the night sky is dark, it is speckled with stars and planets that can be photographed if you set your camera for long exposure times.

Photographing the North Star
One star that most people are familiar with is Polaris, the North Star. For centuries sailors used Polaris to

navigate because it stays very nearly in one place while other stars seem to circle it. If you have a 35-mm camera, you can record on ISO 400 black-and-white film the path of the stars around Polaris. To do this, load your camera with the film, set it on a tripod, and aim it directly at the North Star on a moonless night. Set the camera's focus on infinity and the time exposure at "b." Insert the cable release and leave the shutter open for various time periods.

If you live within 30 mi (50 km) of a large city, 90 min is probably the maximum exposure time for your camera. City lights illuminate the sky artificially, "polluting" the sky and making it difficult to see stars, particularly those near the horizon.

After you have developed the photographs, can you determine the exposure time from the star trails? Is it true that it takes the earth 1h to rotate 15 degrees? Is Polaris at the exact center of the star trails you have photographed? If not, can you explain why?

Photos of the Moon

After you have learned how to take good photographs of the star trails about Polaris, you might enjoy photographing the moon, as well as satellites and a variety of constellations.

Is it true that the apparent angular diameter of the moon is ½ degree? How can you determine the moon's angular diameter photographically?

The sun has very nearly the same angular diameter as the moon. (**Don't look directly at the sun. It can damage your eyes.**) How can this be if the sun is 370 times farther away from the earth than the moon?

When the lower edge of the sun or moon is just touching the horizon, how long will it be before its top edge dips from sight?

Photographing with Color Film

What do you observe about the star trails if you use color-sensitive film? Can you explain your observations?

Circumpolar Constellations

The constellations around Polaris are called circumpolar. In much of the Northern Hemisphere these constellations never set but are visible throughout the night every season of the year. To watch the movement of these constellations, such as the Big and Little Dippers, aim your camera at Polaris as before, but this time open the shutter for a period of only 10 s. Then, without closing the shutter, cover the lens with a black hat for about 4 min. Remove the hat and leave the shutter open for a half hour. This will enable you to obtain prints showing the constellations, followed by 1-degree spaces, followed by 7.5-degree-long star trails.

Mapping Venus*

Venus is the brightest object in the natural sky except for the sun or moon, so it should be easy to find. Your newspaper or an almanac will provide some information about the position of this planet. Often it can be seen after sunset or before sunrise, but there will be times when you'll not be able to see Venus even though the weather is clear.

When the planet is visible, use an astrolabe or other measuring device to establish the angle between Venus and the sun. Since celestial bodies appear to move around Earth once every day, you know that the sun, moon, and stars travel across the sky at a rate of 15 degrees per hour, or 360 degrees in 24 h. Therefore, if you want to measure the angle between Venus and the sun or moon before sunrise or moonrise, or after

[17]

sunset or moonset, you'll need to take into account the angle of the sun or moon below the horizon. For example, if an hour has passed since sunset, then the sun has traveled 15 degrees along its path since it disappeared below the horizon.

Measure the angles between Venus and several distant stars as frequently as possible. What is the maximum angle that you find between Venus and the sun? Between Venus and each of the distant stars?

You may want to photograph Venus and Mars with a camera and tripod. Center the planet you are photographing in the finder, focus on infinity, open the diaphragm to its maximum setting, and take some pictures using different exposures. Keep a record of what you have done so that when you develop the film, you'll know the best exposure to use in future photographs.

Take similar photographs at approximately one-week intervals for a month or more. After you have developed the film, pick out several distant stars visible in each photograph. What do you notice about the motion of Venus or Mars relative to the distant stars?

Use your photos to plot the path of Venus or Mars among the distant stars. Do either of the planets show retrograde (backward) motion relative to the distant stars?

If you view Venus periodically through a telescope or binoculars, you will notice that it goes through phase changes similar to those of the moon. Use the data you collect to construct models that explain the motion of Venus in the sky. In one model, assume that all celestial bodies orbit Earth. In another model, assume that Earth and Venus orbit the sun. You can also assume that distant stars are so far away that all sight lines from Earth to any such star are parallel.

POLARIS AND EARTH'S LATITUDE

You may have heard that the altitude of the North Star, as measured from the horizon, is equal to the latitude of the location from which you observe this star. This means that if you stood at the North Pole (latitude 90 degrees), Polaris would be overhead. At the equator, Polaris would be on the horizon, and at latitude 45 degrees the same star would be 45 degrees above the horizon. Design a method to test this statement and, if you find it to be true, develop an explanation using what you know about astronomy and geometry.

EARTH SATELLITE ORBITS

The laws of physics make it clear that satellites in orbit about the earth must follow elliptical or circular paths. Yet, when you see the paths of satellites mapped on a world map, as shown in Figure 1, the satellites seem to follow an S-shaped path. Why is this? What path would we see on a world map for satellites in polar orbit about the Earth?

UFOs: FACT OR FICTION?

A few years ago, people in the Westchester County area, north of New York City, reported seeing large, unidentified flying objects during the evening hours. An investigation revealed that frequently a group of small planes were found flying in formation during those same hours. The colored lights from these planes looked like a large flying saucer when viewed from the ground.

Investigate some recent UFO sightings. Talk to people who claim to have seen UFOs or to have had

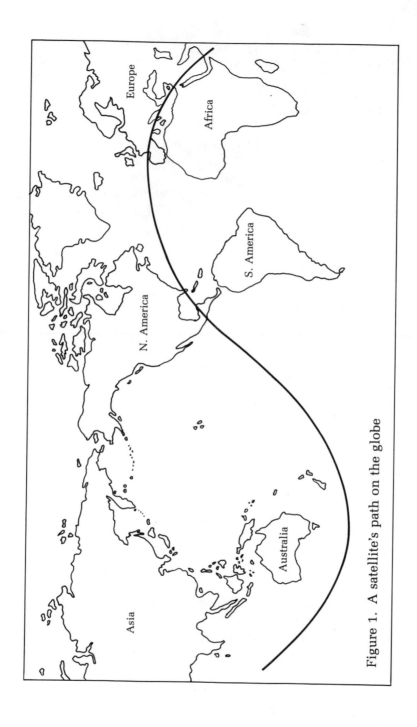

Figure 1. A satellite's path on the globe

contact with the creatures who came from UFOs. Are there natural explanations for the things they saw? Before making a thorough study, you might read issues of *The Skeptical Inquirer*, a magazine published by the Committee for the Scientific Investigation of Claims of the Paranormal, and books on the subject of UFOs, of which there are many.

THE SOLAR CONSTANT

The energy that we receive from the sun varies from day to day depending on the season, the amount of cloud cover, air pollution, and other factors. But just above our atmosphere, the radiant energy that we receive from the sun per area per time is very nearly constant. It is 1.95 cal/cm^2/min or 1,380 W/m^2.

Design a method that will enable you to find out how much of that solar power per area reaches your part of the earth at any given time. You will need to devise some means of absorbing the solar energy over a given area so that you can measure the energy falling on a unit area per unit time.

How do your values compare with the solar constant? How do your measurements compare when you determine the solar power per area at different times of the day? During different seasons? On days when the visibility differs? On cloudy versus clear days?

If possible, use your method for measuring solar power in different parts of the country or world. Where in the country or world would solar power be a feasible energy alternative?

HOW BRIGHT IS THE MOON?

You know that you can see much better at night when the moon is full, but just how bright is the moon? And how does the amount of sunlight reflected from the moon to the earth depend on the phase of the moon?

A photometer can be used to establish the moon's brightness relative to a known source such as a light bulb. You might, for example, allow the moon and a small light bulb to cast two shadows of a stick side by side on a white paper screen. With such a photometer you can move the bulb until the moon's shadow, which the bulb illuminates, has the same darkness as the shadow cast by the bulb's light, which is illuminated by the moon. Then you can measure the distance between the light bulb and the shadows. The intensity of the light from the bulb and the moon are now the same.

You could also use a photometer consisting of a pair of paraffin blocks with a sheet of aluminum foil between them. With a light bulb illuminating one side of the block "sandwich" and the moon illuminating the other, you can move the blocks between moon and bulb until both blocks have the same brightness. At that point, you can be sure that the intensity of the light falling on the blocks from the moon and the light bulb are the same.

On the package in which you purchased the bulb, you can find the bulb's wattage and its efficiency in lumens per watt. Use that information, together with the distance of the bulb from your photometer, to determine the brightness of the moon.

How does the moon's brightness vary from first quarter to last quarter? How does the distance of the moon from the earth affect its brightness?

AN OPTICAL MICROMETER

A mirror can be used to build an optical micrometer that will allow you to measure the thickness of very thin objects, such as a piece of paper. The device is shown in Figure 2. To see how sensitive it is, hold the micrometer so that you can see the reference nail's image in the mirror. Next, line up the thread with the nail's image and mark the position of the thread on the masking tape. Now, carefully insert a small piece of paper between the mirror and the glass plate. Again, align the thread with the image of the reference nail and make a new mark. How does the distance between the marks compare with the thickness of the paper?

To calibrate your micrometer, insert objects of known thickness between the mirror and the glass plate and write the appropriate values on the masking tape to establish a scale. If you measure the thickness of a thick pad of paper, and then divide that length by the number of sheets in the pad, you will have the thickness of one sheet. You can then use one or more sheets to calibrate your instrument. Repeat your calibration to see how precise the device is.

Once it's calibrated, use the micrometer to measure a number of thin objects—heavy and light aluminum foil, hair, tissue paper, thread, etc.

A RANGEFINDER

How can you convert your optical micrometer to a rangefinder that will allow you to measure the distance to objects as far away as a kilometer (0.6 mi) or more? You'll probably want to use the fact that a very distant object is so far away that sight lines to it are essentially parallel even when the sight lines are 100 yd (m) or so apart. On the other hand, sight lines to nearer objects will appear to shift when viewed from the ends of a baseline where sightings to very distant objects are made.

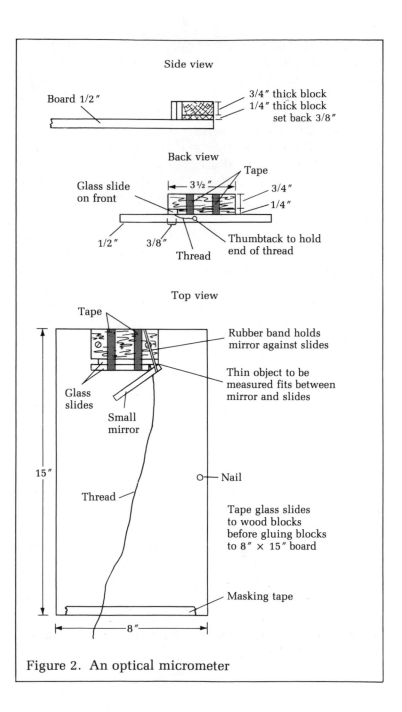

Figure 2. An optical micrometer

INDEX OF REFRACTION
AND DENSITY

When light passes from air to a transparent material, the index of refraction, n, of the material is defined as:

$$n = \sin i / \sin r,$$

where i is the angle of incidence, r is the angle of refraction, and n is a constant for any given material for all incident angles.

With a semicircular cheesebox (or transparent blocks, half cylinders, and empty transparent plastic boxes) and a light box (Figure 3), you can easily measure the index of refraction for a variety of transparent materials, as shown in Figure 4. Both angles i and r are measured between a line perpendicular to the surface at the point of refraction and the light rays. For solids, you might use glass and various plastics. Liquids might include water, alcohol, saturated salt solutions, antifreeze, mineral oil, and any other nontoxic liquids that won't react with the plastic cheesebox. Measure the index of refraction for these various substances and determine the density of each substance in g/cm³. Then see if the index is related to the density of the materials. If you find no relationship, try a graph of the indexes as a function of the molecular weights of the substances.

GLASS, AIR, AND ICE LENSES

As you probably know, a double convex glass lens will cause light to converge, while a concave lens will diverge light. The formula that enables lens makers to determine the focal length of lenses is

$$\frac{1}{f} = (n-1)(\frac{1}{R_1} - \frac{1}{R_2}),$$

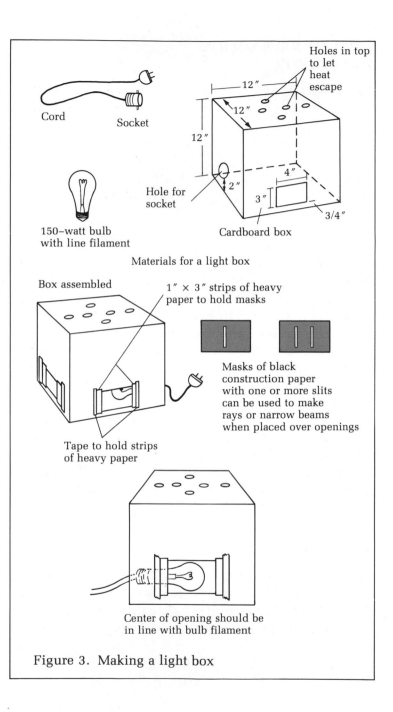

Cord Socket

Holes in top to let heat escape

12″
12″
12″

Hole for socket 2″
4″
3″
3/4″

150–watt bulb with line filament

Cardboard box

Materials for a light box

Box assembled

1″ × 3″ strips of heavy paper to hold masks

Masks of black construction paper with one or more slits can be used to make rays or narrow beams when placed over openings

Tape to hold strips of heavy paper

Center of opening should be in line with bulb filament

Figure 3. Making a light box

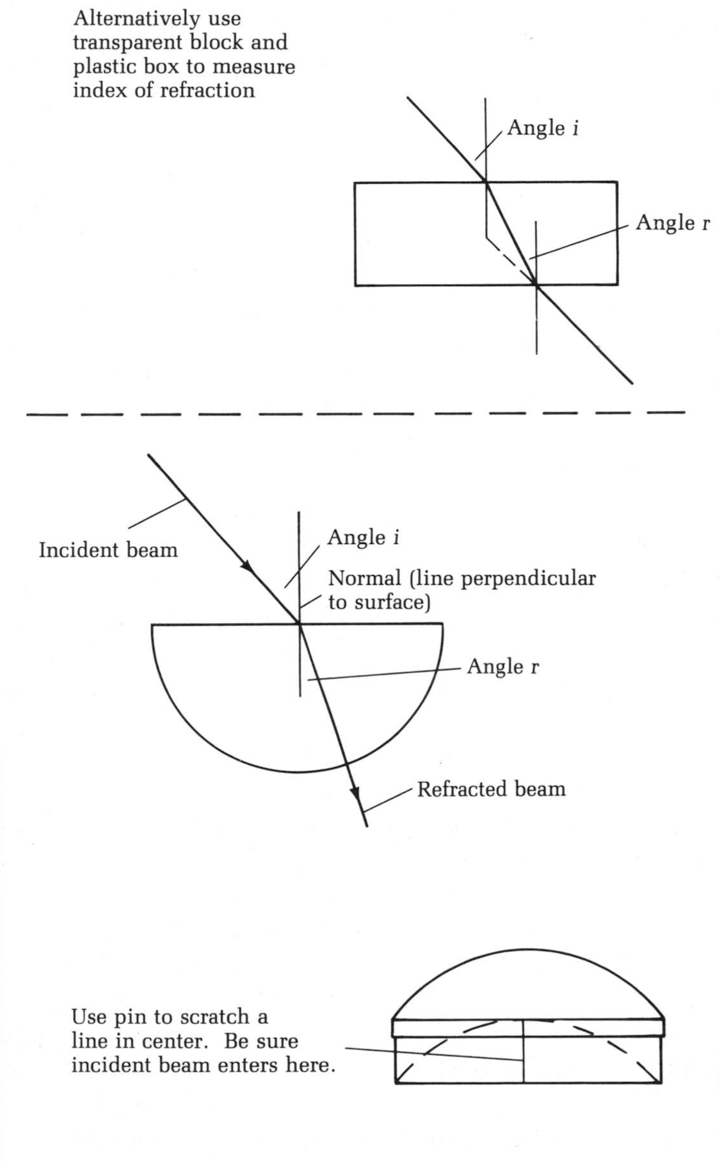

Alternatively use transparent block and plastic box to measure index of refraction

Angle *i*

Angle *r*

Incident beam

Angle *i*

Normal (line perpendicular to surface)

Angle *r*

Refracted beam

Use pin to scratch a line in center. Be sure incident beam enters here.

Figure 4. Measuring the index of refraction

where R_1 and R_2 are the radii of the spherical surfaces of the two sides of the lens, f is the focal length of the lens, and n is the index of refraction of the transparent material used to make the lens. Is the number 1 in $(n-1)$ the index of refraction of air, or is it a pure number?

What would happen if you made an air lens and placed it in water? The value of n would now be 1 because the index of refraction of air is 1. But the index of refraction of water is 1.33. Does this mean the $(n-1)$ value in the lens maker's formula would now be $(1-1.33)$, or would it be $1-1(0)$? If it's 0, what would f be? If it's $1-1.33$, then $1/f$ has become a negative value. Would a double-convex air lens then diverge light? Would a double-concave air lens converge light?

To find out, seal two watch glasses together with plastic electrical tape as shown in Figure 5 and place the air lens you've made in a beaker of water. Place a point source of light some distance from the beaker. You can use a clear bulb with a line filament. By placing the bulb so that the end of the filament is turned toward the beaker, you will have a point of light. Cover the side of the beaker nearest the light with black paper in which you have cut a pair of narrow slits. Tape a white paper screen on the other side of the beaker. By looking at the images of the slits on the screen, you'll be able to tell whether the air lens diverges or converges the light. What do you find?

Can you use these air lenses to make real and virtual images under water? How does the focal length of a glass or plastic lens in water compare with its focal length in air? Does the lens maker's formula still apply?

Try to make a lens from ice. You're more likely to have success if you use water that has been boiled. In that way most of the air dissolved in the water will have been removed. What can you use for a mold?

[28]

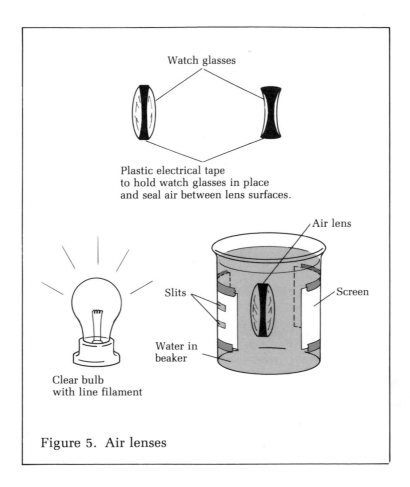

Figure 5. Air lenses

CYLINDRICAL LENSES

When lenses are made, the surfaces of the lenses are like partial surfaces of spheres. If the curvature of a lens is limited to two dimensions instead of three, cylindrical lenses are obtained. A jar filled with water constitutes a cylindrical lens. If you place such a lens in a beam of light as shown in Figure 6, you can see how the lens affects the path of the light beam. With a pair of parallel light rays from a light box, you can easily measure the focal length of a cylindrical lens.

[29]

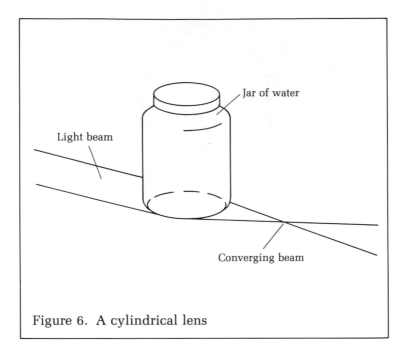

Figure 6. A cylindrical lens

How is the focal length of the lens affected by the diameter of the cylinder? If you let the light rays from a light box pass through colored filters, you can see if the focal length is affected by the color of the light. What do you find?

Using cylindrical lenses, develop some demonstrations that you or your teacher can use to help other students understand how convex lenses create real and virtual images.

Can you use cylindrical lenses to diverge light?

THE SPEED OF LIGHT*

Nearly 400 years ago Galileo tried to measure the speed of light. He and a friend stood on mountaintops several miles apart, holding lanterns. When Galileo opened his lantern, allowing its light to shine forth, his friend was instructed to respond by opening his own lantern as soon as he saw the light. What Galileo found was that the time interval in spotting the light from the distant lantern was no longer than the reaction time of his friend. His results led Galileo to think that perhaps the speed of light was infinite.

Later, during the nineteenth century, Fizeau, Michelson, and others measured the speed of light and found it to be fast but finite. See if you can measure the speed of light with electronic equipment or by other means.

**The Speed of Light
in Different Media**
Most high school or college physics textbooks and laboratory manuals describe a method that will enable you to find the wavelength of light. It can be done with two narrow slits that are very close together as described in the laboratory guide that accompanies *PSSC Physics* by Haber Schaim, et al. The experiment is referred to as "Young's experiment" because it was first done by Thomas Young around 1800.

The wavelength can be determined more accurately in a similar experiment using a diffraction grating, as described in many secondary school and college physics textbooks, such as *Modern Physics* by J.E. Williams, et al. The relationship for finding the wavelength is the same, but the distance between the slits that give rise to the interference pattern is much smaller in the diffraction grating than in the double slits used in the Young experiment.

Once you've found the wavelength of light in air, you can determine the speed of light in any medium relative to the speed of light in air, which is 3.0×10^8 m/s. Just compare the wavelength of light in air with the wavelength of the same light in a different medium. For example, as you can see in Figure 7, the wavelength of light can be determined in water using a fish tank, a line source of light such as a showcase bulb, a diffraction grating, a ruler, and some measuring tape.

The speed of light (c) is given by the product of the wavelength and the frequency ($c = f\lambda$). Since the frequency of light of a particular color is always the same, the speed of light will be proportional to its wavelength. By measuring the wavelength of a particular color of light in different media, including air, you can determine the ratio of the speed of light in the two media:

*wavelength in air/wavelength in medium =
speed in air/speed in medium*

What is the speed of light in water according to your measurements?

Is the speed of light in water different from the speed of light in seawater? How about the speed of light in alcohol? Is the speed of light in a medium related to the index of refraction of the medium?

FIBER OPTICS*

When light travels from glass to air, all the light will be reflected back into the glass if the light strikes the boundary between glass and air at an angle greater than the critical angle. That is, if $\sin \phi_{air}$ in the equation

$$\sin \phi_{glass} \times n_{glass} = \sin \phi_{air} \times 1$$

is greater than 1, then ϕ_{air} exceeds 90 degrees and all the light will be reflected back into the glass as shown in Figure 8a. No light will enter the air. This phenomenon is called total internal reflection.

[32]

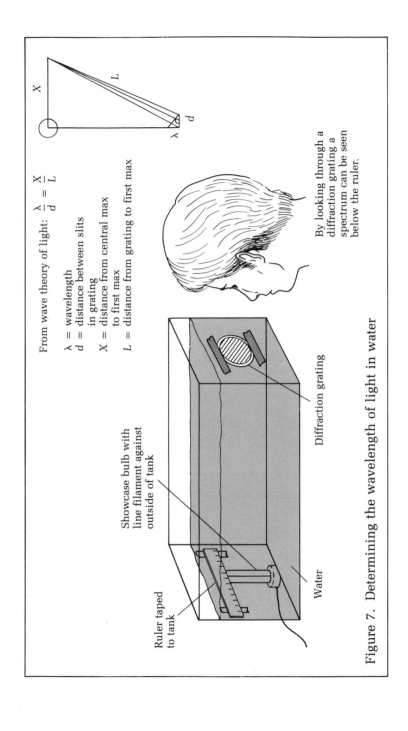

From wave theory of light: $\dfrac{\lambda}{d} = \dfrac{X}{L}$

λ = wavelength
d = distance between slits in grating
X = distance from central max to first max
L = distance from grating to first max

By looking through a diffraction grating a spectrum can be seen below the ruler.

Ruler taped to tank

Showcase bulb with line filament against outside of tank

Diffraction grating

Water

Figure 7. Determining the wavelength of light in water

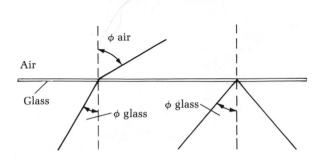

ϕ air

Air

Glass

ϕ glass

ϕ glass

At the critical angle, sin ϕ
air becomes 1.0 and all the
light is reflected within the glass

Figure 8a. The critical angle

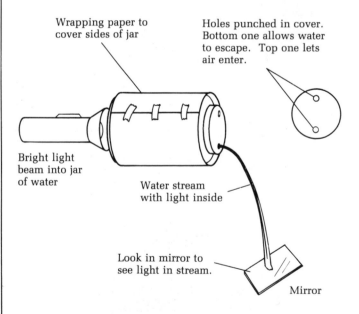

Wrapping paper to
cover sides of jar

Holes punched in cover.
Bottom one allows water
to escape. Top one lets
air enter.

Bright light
beam into jar
of water

Water stream
with light inside

Look in mirror to
see light in stream.

Mirror

Figure 8b. Total internal reflection in a stream of water

You can see this effect for yourself by setting up the demonstration shown in Figure 8b. Light will follow the stream of water emerging from the bottle. By holding a mirror in the stream, you can see that light is following the path of the water stream.

Doctors make use of the principle of total internal reflection when they look inside the human body using optic fibers. Such a view allows them to do surgery with very small incisions. Many knee operations are done by making a small cut into which optic fibers are inserted so that the surgeon can look into the joint and remove loose cartilage or repair torn ligaments.

Using optic fibers that you can buy from a science supply company or a novelty store, build a periscope that can be used to see around corners. As you become more accomplished in handling these fibers, see if you can build a light tube that will enable you to look for sunken ocean treasures or peer into deep, dark caves.

Many scientists believe that optic fibers will become increasingly important in communication because light pulses can be used to send messages more efficiently than electric currents. Perhaps you can develop a way to use optic fibers to transmit telephone messages. If you succeed in that venture, you might try developing a photophone that enables you to see, as well as talk to, whoever answers your call.

WHY ARE FOG LIGHTS YELLOW?

Some cars have fog lights as well as headlights. Look closely and you will see that the light coming from many fog lights is yellow. If you contact a company that manufactures fog lights, you will probably be told that yellow light penetrates fog better than white light because the longer wavelengths of yellow light are scattered less than the shorter blue and green wavelengths in ordinary white light.

Is this really true? Conduct your own tests to see if yellow light passes through fog better than white light. Does the size of the water droplets in the fog have any effect on the wavelength of the light scattered most?

A FISH'S-EYE VIEW OF THE WORLD*

A fish, looking through the surface of the water from below, has a very different view of the world than you do. Light traveling from objects on land to the fish's eye is refracted (bent) as it passes from air into water. At the same time, light coming from objects beneath the water is reflected, often totally if its angle exceeds the critical angle, from the water's surface.

To see the world from a fish's view, you might like to look at the world above from beneath the surface of a swimming pool. For the best results, the surface of the water should be very calm. To show others what you have seen, you can take pictures from beneath the surface with a waterproof camera or movie camera. You should not try such an experiment unless you are an accomplished swimmer and have an adult to assist you. **Do not connect your camera to an electrical outlet or use any high-voltage source while under water.**

This is not an easy project to do, but the resulting views can be phenomenal. Seat some friends along the edge of the pool with their feet in the water. You'll notice that as you move slowly under the water, your friends' feet will seem to separate from their legs and appear inverted in another position. What other strange views can you see?

[36]

2

EARTH, WATER, SEA, AND AIR

Aristotle and other Greek philosophers believed there were four elements: earth, air, fire, and water. We know now that none of these are elements in a chemical sense, but we are still surrounded by these "elements," and while our sense of what these substances are has changed, they still encompass a lot of science.

WHAT'S IN THE AIR?

The air over cities is quite different from the air over farmland. Both contain about the same percentage of oxygen and nitrogen, but the tiny particles that "float" in these gases are quite different.

Before collecting some air samples, coat a few microscope slides with petroleum jelly. Place different slides in various locations for several hours. Then collect the slides and examine each one under a microscope. See if you can identify the particles—soil, soot, sand, pollen, etc.—that collect on each slide. You can use your slides to estimate the ratio of the concentration of various kinds of particles in the air.

Use a vacuum cleaner to make more quantitative measurements. First, determine how much air per minute passes through the vacuum cleaner by collecting, in a large, empty, trash bag, the air emerging from its exhaust vent. Then, from the volume of air collected in a fixed time, calculate the rate that air flows through the machine.

Use tape to hold a vaseline-coated microscope slide over the opening where the intake hose attaches to the machine. Part of the entering air will flow over the slide. Remeasure the volume of air that flows through the machine each minute with the slide in place.

Use the vacuum to draw samples of air over slides you have prepared. Collect numerous samples under various weather conditions and at different seasons of the year. After collecting a sample, remove the slide and add a cover slip.

Examine each slide under a microscope. If possible, photograph the slides through a microscope. Determine the total area of the slide where particles collected. What fraction of this area is visible under the microscope? For each slide determine the average number of particles visible in a field of view after examining several different positions on the slide. Then calculate the number of particles collected on each slide.

What fraction of the air stream hit the slide? What is the number of particles per volume of air? How is the number of particles per volume related to weather conditions? To location? To the season?

WATCHING THE WEATHER

By making careful daily readings of instruments and observing the sky overhead, you may become adept at predicting the weather. Keep your records on a chart. Include the time and date that you make each reading or observation of temperature, air pressure, humidity, wind speed and direction, rainfall, fire hazard, cloud cover and appearance, and the "feel" of the air (damp, cool, warm, etc.).

To measure temperature, use an outdoor thermometer that is not in direct sunlight. You might like to use an indoor–outdoor thermometer and a maximum–minimum thermometer if available. An *aneroid barometer* can be used to measure air pressure. Pay particular attention to changes in pressure. A wet-and-dry-bulb thermometer can be used to measure relative humidity, or you may prefer to measure the dew point to determine both relative and absolute humidity. Make a weather vane to measure wind direction and an anemometer to measure wind speed. How can you calibrate your anemometer?

How can you measure rainfall? Fire hazard?

After a few months, try to predict the weather based on your measurements and observations. Make your prediction before listening to one on radio or TV. How do your predictions compare with those made by meteorologists? Do you get better with practice?

HAZE AND HUMIDITY

The view of nearby mountains may reveal a silhouette of soft green velvet against a bright blue sky when the relative humidity is low. Several days later, when the relative humidity is more than 90 percent, these same mountains may be barely visible through haze.

Is haze related to humidity? Can the humidity be determined from the visibility range?

UNDERGROUND WATER*

Thirty times as much water resides in underground sources, called *aquifers*, as in lakes, ponds, and rivers.

[39]

This water fills the spaces between rocks and soil particles. The top of an aquifer constitutes the water table; the bottom is bounded by bedrock. Gravity causes water to move slowly along an aquifer at a rate determined by the steepness of the bedrock.

Some deep aquifers are heated by the earth's core and produce hot springs where they discharge. Other aquifers lead to springs, lakes, or rivers. By digging or drilling wells, water can be pumped from an aquifer.

Geologists trace the movement of water in aquifers with colored salts or soluble radioactive compounds. To trace the movement of water in an aquifer near your home, you might contact a geologist at a college or university, or one connected with the state or federal government. Perhaps he or she will welcome your assistance.

In many aquifers, water is being removed faster than it is being replenished by rainfall. As a result, the water table is falling. The Ogallala aquifer, which extends from South Dakota to Texas, is being mined for irrigation at a rate that exceeds its natural rate of replenishment. You might like to investigate water table levels over this or other aquifers. Can you suggest ways to bring an aquifer into equilibrium if it is being depleted?

HARD AND SOFT WATER

Because underground water is in contact with soil and rock particles, it usually contains calcium and magnesium salts. Soap added to such water combines with these ions to form a gummy precipitate instead of cleansing suds. Until these ions are removed, the soap cannot be used for cleaning purposes. Water that contains an abundance of calcium and magnesium ions and does not readily form suds with soap is called *hard* water. It is so named because it is "hard" to get a lather with soap in such water. Hard water also causes scale to form on the inside of pipes, tanks, and radiators through which it flows. On the other hand, soft water forms so many suds that it makes rinsing difficult. Further, the minerals in hard water make it more healthful for drinking purposes.

To establish a standard sample of water for hardness, add distilled water to a test tube until it is one-third full. Then add one to five drops of liquid soap. The exact number depends on the concentration of the soap you use. Use enough drops so that after shaking the tube for 20 s the layer of suds does not quite reach the top of the tube.

To test a water sample for hardness, add the same number of drops of soap that you added to the distilled water standard, stopper the tube, and shake it for 20 s. Hold the tube upright and measure the thickness of the suds above the water. The higher the layer of suds, the softer the water.

Obtain a variety of water samples. You might obtain local samples from rain water, a river, pond, lake, reservoir, tap, etc. During travels you might collect samples from various cities, rivers, lakes, and the ocean.

Run the test three times on each sample and record your results, How does each sample compare with the distilled water standard? Are any of the samples as soft as the distilled water? What is the hardest water? Where was it found? Can you explain where its hardness comes from?

Design tests that will enable you to identify the particular ions and their concentrations in each sample. For example, chloride ions, which are commonly found in hard water, can be identified by adding silver ions that lead to the formation of a precipitate of white silver chloride.

SOAP FILMS AND
BUBBLES THAT LAST

Most soap bubbles are ephemeral, but with patience you can make and watch soap films and bubbles that last for hours, not seconds.

Here are some recipes for making long lasting soap films. The first one was proposed by Bernard Sharkey of Berkeley, Michigan; the second by Paul Smith in a science fair project more than 35 years ago; the third is of unknown origin.

1) Mix together:
   8 oz (240 mL) of soft or distilled water,
   2½ oz (75 mL) of Joy liquid detergent,
   6½ oz (200 mL) of glycerine.

2) Mix together in the following order:
   2 oz (60 mL) of tap water,
   1 tablespoonful (15 mL) of pure gelatin.

   Mix and heat to 190°F (90°C) in a double boiler. Dissolve gelatin and let bubbles rise. Then add:

   ⅓ oz (9 mL) of glycerin and ⅑ oz (3 mL) of Joy liquid detergent.

   Stir gently to avoid formation of foam.

3) Make a mixture consisting of one-third glycerin and two-thirds Joy liquid detergent.

- Which of these recipes seems to produce the longest lasting bubbles? The longest lasting soap films?
- Try making recipes of your own and see how long you can preserve these soap films and bubbles.

[42]

- Large, flat sheets of bubble film can be made by dipping a wire ring into the solutions. How large can you make these sheets? Does the area of the film affect its "life"?

- Bubbles blown with these soaps can be kept suspended on 3- x 5-in. file cards. A damp spot at the center of the card will hold them in place until they dry.

- When soap films or bubbles drain to a thickness that is equal to, or less than, one-quarter the wavelength of visible light, they become dark and no longer show the colored interference fringes that characterize ordinary soap films.

- Devise a way to measure the thickness of soap films and bubbles.

- How thick are soap films and bubbles when first made? How thick are they after drying?

- How can you make soap bubbles that will float in air?

FROM SNOWFALL TO RAINFALL

You may have heard that 10 in (25 cm) of snowfall is equivalent to 1 in (2.5 cm) of rainfall. But doesn't it depend on the kind of snowfall?

To find out, you can take fresh samples of different types of newly fallen snow, measure the depth of the sample, let it melt, and measure the depth of the water that remains after melting.

To measure how many inches or centimeters of water can be obtained from a given snowfall, press the open end of a clear plastic cylinder into the newly fallen snow until the bottom of the cylinder is just above the snow. Be sure you do not compress the snow. Reach under the snow and slide a flat object, such as a sheet of cardboard, over the open end of the cylinder. Remove the cylinder from the snow, turn it right side up, and mark the depth of the snow. After the snow has melted in the covered vial, measure the depth of the water.

Repeat this procedure for a variety of snow types —light, heavy, sleet, etc. How many inches of snow would have been required to produce 1 in of rainfall from each sample? How many cubic feet of water per acre would be provided by each of the snowstorms from which you took samples?

THE ACID RAIN DEBATE*

You have probably read that acid rain, which many claim is the result of the sulfur and nitrogen oxides generated by industrial plants, is devastating forests and lakes in North America. However, in *The Great Acid Rain Mystery* (published by Hudson Institute, 5395 Emerson Way, Indianapolis, IN 46226), William M. Brown raises questions about this issue. He states that "there is no clear and unambiguous cause-and-effect relationship that makes acid rain undeniably guilty of any of the major accusations which have been leveled against it."

Can you find unambiguous evidence that acid rain is guilty of the devastating effects claimed by many environmentalists? If not, what is causing reduced fish and tree populations in many areas of the world?

A SALTWATER AQUARIUM

Build and stock a saltwater aquarium. You may think this is a fairly simple project, but the problems involved in maintaining fresh, clean, cold water when the tank contains sea life is not as easy as you may

[44]

think. You will need ocean water or artificial sea salts, a good filter, and a supply of plants and animals that can live together in salt water.

While the challenge of establishing a saltwater aquarium is a demanding one, the aquarium, once established, will provide hours of interesting observations and learning.

Can you establish a population of plants and animals that sustains itself so that you do not have to provide food? If you succeed, what is the food chain in the aquarium?

Can freshwater plants or animals adjust to a saltwater environment if the transition is done slowly?

Is it true that the concentration of salt in seawater is comparable to the concentration of salt in the body fluids of land animals?

DISAPPEARING BEACHES*

The August 10th, 1987, issue of Time contains an article entitled "Where's the Beach" that discusses the problem of beach erosion along the coasts of the United States. While you probably can't find a way to stop the rising level of the world's oceans, you may be able to design some way of reducing beach erosion along our coasts. For example, in some places stone jetties, perpendicular to the shore, are built to reduce the movement of sand. In other places, beach grass is planted to hold soil in place. Do any of these methods work? Can you devise better ones?

SOIL AND WATER

Some kinds of soil hold water well; other types allow water to pass through quite rapidly. To study the effect of soil on water retention, set up some large plastic containers as shown in Figure 9. Place a collecting vessel beneath each container. Into each container put a different soil. You might use sand, gravel, loam, clay, and various combinations of these soils. Add the same volume of water to the top of each container and measure the rate at which water passes through each type of soil.

Which type of soil(s) would be best for growing plants? For a septic system? For an athletic field?

Another approach would be to gather soils from different places such as meadows, forests, marshes, gravel banks, and lawns. Weigh out equal amounts of each type of soil and place them on aluminum pie tins. Dry each sample in bright sunlight or in an oven until no further weight loss occurs. Which soil sample held the most water? The least?

Are your findings related to the amount of plant life found in the original samples?

DECAY FACTORS

The breakdown of organic matter in the earth gives rise to humus, which provides growing plants with minerals and other essential materials. Often gardeners will prepare a humus pile from leaves, grass, garbage, and other organic matter. Left for a period of time, this matter, when added to garden soil, will accelerate the rate at which plants grow.

To investigate some of the factors affecting the breakdown of organic matter into humus, fill five clay pots with topsoil. Bury a cube of potato, 1 in (2–3 cm) on a side, in each pot. Leave the soil in one pot dry. Keep the soil in the other four pots moist. Incubate one of them in a 400°F oven for several hours. Keep another in the refrigerator. Place a third pot in a warm, sunny place. Put the remaining pot in a warm, dark environment together with the pot that was heated in the oven.

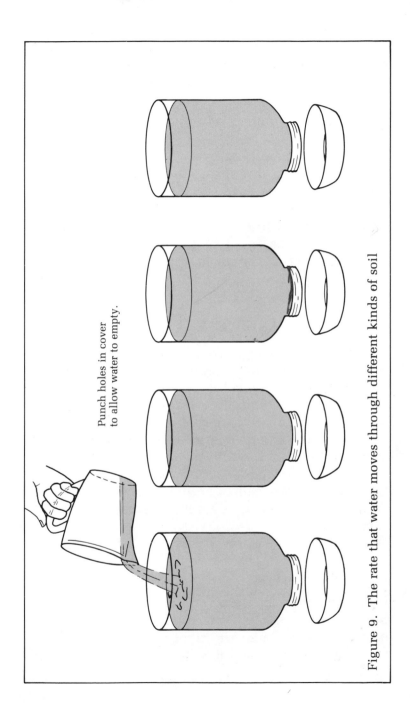

Punch holes in cover
to allow water to empty.

Figure 9. The rate that water moves through different kinds of soil

Examine the buried pieces of potatoes periodically to determine which environment seems to produce the most rapid rate of decay into humus.

ROADSIDE GEOLOGY

Find places where a highway has been made by cutting and blasting through rock. How many different kinds of rock do you see? How can you identify these rocks by testing?

Are there any fossils? Any artifacts of human existence from the past?

Try to explain the geological history of the rocks you see.

FOOD CHAINS AND WEBS

Select a bush or a small tree for your study. Examine the tree or bush and the ground around it. Look for other plants or animals that live on it. Try to identify each species you find. Can you find webs? Egg clusters? Evidence of animals that come and go?

How do matter and energy pass through this plant? How do the plants and animals that you find on or around the plant under study use the plant in their lives? What food chains and food webs can you find? What adaptations are evident? Which species are competing? Which are coexisting?

A FOSSIL HUNT

Plants and animals decay rapidly so that usually only hard parts such as teeth, bones, shells, or woody tissue become fossils. Under the right conditions, however, tissue as soft as that of a jellyfish has been preserved.

You may be able to find the remains of entire plants or animals or their imprints in ancient rocks. Can you identify the plants or animals? Can you determine present-day plants or animals that evolved from these ancestors?

You might also find ancient insects that were trapped in coniferous tree sap. When the sap changed into amber, the insects were preserved as fossils.

Sometimes ancient animals left tracks that were preserved, such as the dinosaur tracks in the Connecticut Valley or in the foothills west of Denver, Colorado. Perhaps you'll be able to find such fossilized tracks, or with some digging you might find the remains of an Indian camp or village from several centuries ago. There are a number of such digs in various parts of the country where you might find an opportunity to work with an anthropologist. A fairly extensive Indian dig is located in Washington, Connecticut.

A UNIVERSE OF SPIRALS

The spiral is a shape common to earth and beyond. The nautilus, a ram's horns, snail shells, the tendrils on climbing plants, water entering a drain, hurricanes threatening our coasts, even many galaxies—including our own, the Milky Way—have a spiral shape.

Is the widespread occurrence of this shape an accident, or is there something about the spiral that has caused nature and evolution to favor it?

Do other shapes such as triangles or circles occur commonly in nature? If so, what is so special about them? What advantage do they offer over other shapes?

Among higher animals, bilateral symmetry seems to predominate over spiral or radial symmetry. What evolutionary advantages does bilateral symmetry offer?

THE SHAKING EARTH

Geologists use seismographs to detect earthquakes and other large disturbances such as nuclear explosions. You can build a small seismograph as shown in Figure 10. About 1 ft (30 cm) of a ¾-in piece of pipe, with female threads uppermost, should be embedded in a slab of concrete. If possible, the slab should rest on bedrock so that small vibrations such as those caused by passing cars do not affect the seismograph. A second piece of pipe, about 3 ft (90 cm) long, can be threaded into the shorter pipe that is firmly fixed to the conrete slab.

Have a skilled adult use a drill to make a dimple (depression) in the vertical pipe. The adult can also grind one end of a metal rod, about 3 ft (90 cm) long, to fit into the dimple in the vertical pipe. Using strong wire, connect the outer end of the rod to the top of the vertical pipe. Pieces of the same wire can be used to attach weights to the bottom of the rod. A heavy metal plate fastened to the rod and hanging in a pan of oil will reduce the rod's sensitivity if you find it responding to minor vibrations.

Call on the skilled adult to bolt a support for an old alarm clock to the concrete slab. The clock should be firmly fastened to the support with its face very near the end of the horizontal metal rod. After snipping off the clock's minute hand, attach a thin cardboard disk covered with soot to the hour hand. (You can blacken the disk by holding it above a candle flame.) Fasten a stiff wire to the end of the rod so that it just touches the outer edge of the disk.

Any motion of the Earth will cause the slab to move. But the end of a pendulum, in this case the tip of the rod, tends to remain at rest; thus, any motion of the Earth will result in a disturbance in the movement of the wire tip on the smoked disk. The greater the

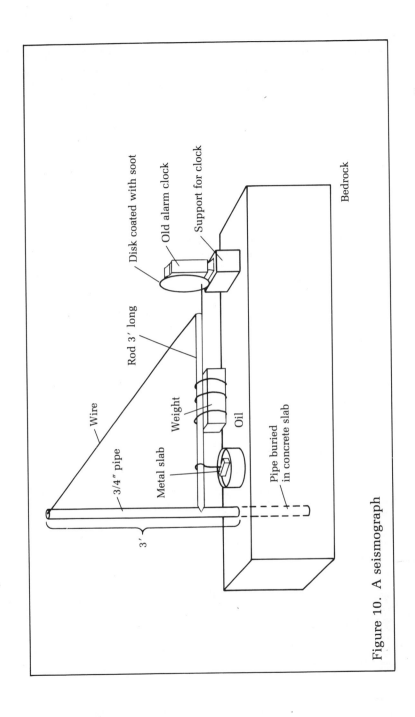

Figure 10. A seismograph

movement, the larger the displacement of the tip from its normal path along the disk.

How would you improve upon the design of this seismograph? For example, how could you modify the design so as to know what time an earthquake occurred? How could you determine the direction of, and distance to, the center of an earthquake? Can you find a way to predict when and where earthquakes will occur?

Can earthquakes be predicted by the behavior of animals? Some people claim that several days before an earthquake animals that normally live underground, such as snakes, mice, and moles, will leave their burrows. Dogs, cats, and other pets, they claim, will become restless and noisy prior to an earthquake. Others believe that water levels in wells will rise a day or two before a quake takes place. Is there any truth to these claims?

What is meant by "earthquake light"? How can you distinguish an earthquake from a sonic boom or an explosion?

3

BODY AND MIND SCIENCE

Most people enjoy doing science projects related to the human mind and body because it helps them to better understand themselves. Try some of these projects and see if you agree.

Should you decide to use one of these projects for a science fair, check the rules to be sure that experiments involving human beings are allowed.

If you ask someone to serve as a subject for one of these projects, be certain that person is in good health.

DO YOU NEED YOUR EYES FOR BODY BALANCE?

Your sense of balance is controlled to a large extent by the semicircular canals in your inner ear. Movement of the fluid and particles in these canals stimulates nerve cells that send impulses to the brain, which in turn sends impulses to your muscles so that you contract and relax the right muscles in order to maintain balance. But do you think your eyes play a role in maintaining body balance?

To find out, stand on one foot in a large open space with your eyes open. Be careful there are no objects on which you might fall and get hurt. Most people can do this quite easily. Now close your eyes and try to stand on one foot. Not as easy, is it? For how long can you balance on one foot with your eyes closed? Do you find it as difficult to do in the dark with your eyes open? Is it easier if you lower your center of gravity by bending your leg? Does it help if you wear high boots tightly laced? If you spread your arms? If you're well rested?

Are some people better at maintaining one-legged balance with closed eyes than others? Do these people tend to be athletes? Are they short in stature? Are they predominantly males or females? Do you detect any patterns that help you to predict whether a person will have good or poor one-legged balance?

PINHOLES AND
UPSIDE-DOWN SHADOW

Make a pinhole in an index card. Hold the pinhole in front of one eye and look at some print on a page in bright light. Can you see the print more clearly through the pinhole? Can you see the print more clearly if you view it through a narrow tube, such as a rolled up sheet of paper?

Move your eye closer to the paper until the print becomes fuzzy. Now place the pinhole close to your eye. Can you read the print now?

Hold the card with the pinhole about a foot from your eye and look through it to a bright patch of white light or the sky, **but do not look at the sun.** With your other hand, carefully hold the sharp end of a straight pin between your thumb and index finger. Move the pin's head slowly up and down just in front of the eye you are using to look through the pinhole. **Be careful. Don't let the pin touch your eye.** The pinhead will cast a shadow on your retina. But notice! The shadow is upside down, and when you move the pinhead down, the shadow moves up. If you move the pinhead up, the shadow moves down.

Why is it that you can read print through a pinhole when you're too close to read it otherwise? Why is the pinhead's shadow, as seen through a pinhole, upside down?

PERIPHERAL VISION AND COLOR

When you see things from the corners of your eyes, the light entering your eyes falls predominantly on the periphery of your retina, where the rod cells are located. For some people, such as basketball players, peripheral vision is a must.

To test a subject for peripheral vision, have him sit at a high table with his chin on his fist while staring straight ahead at a mark placed about 2 m directly in front of the table.

With the subject in place, cover the eye not being tested. Be sure not to apply pressure to the eye. Mount a small colored index card on the end of a measuring stick. Beginning near the ear on either side of the head, slowly move the card, at eye level, forward. Be sure the subject continues to stare straight ahead throughout the experiment. Ask the person to tell you when the front edge of the card is first visible and record the position of the card at that point. Then ask the person to tell you when he can identify the color of the card. You can use a variety of colors, such as blue, green, red, and yellow. Does the color of the card seem to affect the position at which the card is first seen?

Does peripheral vision seem to be related to a subject's sex? Eye color? Age? Athletic experience? Facial shape? Do eyeglasses help or hinder a person's peripheral vision?

OTHER TESTS
OF THE SENSES

- Design a test of your own to measure someone's ability to perceive depth. For example, how far apart do two objects have to be before someone can tell that one is farther away than the other? How do your subjects do if one eye is covered?

- Design a test to measure a person's reaction time to a visual stimulus; that is, how long does it take after something is seen for the subject to make an appropriate response? Design another test to measure reaction time to an auditory stimulus.

- Use solutions applied to various parts of a subject's tongue to map the taste sensations of sweet, salt, sour, and bitter. The solutions can be applied with a cotton-tipped swab. Have the subject rinse his or her mouth with water between tests. Solutions of sugar and quinine, each with a concentration of 0.5%, can be used to test for sweet and bitter tastes, respectively. A solution of one part household vinegar to nine parts water can be used to test for the sour taste. To test for a salty taste, use a 5% salt solution.

    Are all parts of the tongue sensitive to all the tastes, or do different parts of the tongue detect different tastes?

- Can substances be tasted without a sense of smell? To find out, repeat the taste tests, but have the subject pinch both nostrils closed. Blindfold your subject and test to see if he or she can identify or distinguish among the following substances when they are placed on the tongue: a few drops of lukewarm tea and drops of Coke or Pepsi, chopped apple, potato, or onion.

■ Using a compass (dividers or calipers), find out how far apart the points on the compass must be for a blindfolded subject to detect two distinct sensations of touch instead of one. Try touching the subject on the arm, hand, back, neck, and legs. **Be careful not to push the compass points into the subject's skin or draw blood.** Is the ability to detect two separate touch sensations related to the part of the body being tested?

REFLEXES

When you go to a doctor for a physical examination, he or she may use a small mallet to tap your bent leg just below the knee. When this is done, you automatically straighten your leg. This is a reflex action—an automatic muscular response to a stimulus. You can elicit a similar response from a partner. Have that person sit on a table with his or her legs hanging loosely over the table's edge. With the side of your hand, gently tap the tendon just below the kneecap. If you hit the right spot, you will see your partner automatically straighten his or her leg.

Here are several other reflex actions your body performs on "request":

■ *Pupil reflex.* Look at the pupil (black circular area) in the center of someone's eye or look at your own pupil using a mirror. Do this in dim light. What happens to the size of the pupil when bright light is shined onto it? What happens when the bright light is removed?

- *Ciliospinal reflex.* Watch a subject's pupils as you gently move the hairs on the back of his or her neck. What happens to the size of the pupils? What happens to the subject's pupils if you pinch the back of his or her neck?

- *Blinking reflex.* Ask someone to sit quietly in a chair. Without warning, **but with care not to touch the eyes,** wave your hand in front of his or her face. What happens?

- *Salivary reflex.* Don't swallow for a period of 3 min. Then spit the saliva in your mouth into a medicine cup. Ask a partner to place a few drops of lemon juice at various points on your tongue. After a 3-min period, again spit all the saliva in your mouth into a medicine cup. How do the volumes of saliva compare?

  Will drops of orange juice elicit a similar response?

- If you test different people for any of these reflexes, do you note any differences in individual responses? Do some people respond faster than others? Do the responses vary in magnitude?

- Can some people control any of these reflexes? For example, can anyone prevent his or her pupil from dilating in dim light?

- Can you find other body reflexes that are common to all humans?

HICCUPS

When you hiccup, your diaphragm and rib muscles suddenly contract, forcing air from your lungs. The hiccup sound is made when the glottis at the top of your voice box (larynx) closes.

Test the various common cures for hiccups, such as holding your breath, drinking water, being frightened, etc. Which of these cures work? Why do you think they work?

Once you've found one or more cures, see if you can determine what causes hiccups. If there is more than one cause, can you find anything common to all the causes?

YAWNING

We all know that yawning is "contagious." Some people yawn when they read about yawning. Perhaps you're yawning right now!

People used to believe that yawning is the body's response to a need for more oxygen because we tend to yawn when we are tired. But Robert R. Provine of the University of Maryland could find no evidence that yawning was related to the body's oxygen or carbon dioxide level.

If yawning is not related to our need for oxygen, why do we yawn? What causes it? And what purpose, if any, does it serve?

FAST FINGERNAILS?

You know that fingernails grow—you have to keep cutting them. But how fast do they grow?

To find out, use the edge of a fingernail file to make a short, straight line across the base of your thumbnail within the white, semicircular cuticle. Measure the distance from the file mark to the inside edge of the white band at the end of your nail. A week later make the same measurement. The difference between these two measurements will give you the distance your nail grew in one week. Continue measuring your thumbnail's growth each week. Does your thumbnail grow at a constant speed? Do your other fingernails and toenails grow faster or slower than your thumbnail?

Measure the fingernail growth rate of a number of people. Do you find any pattern associated with rate of nail growth? Do the nails of females grow faster than those of males? Does the growth rate slow with age? Does it vary with the season of the year? With the activity level of the subject? With the subject's occupation?

ARE YOU A WATER WITCH?*

Dowsers (often called water witches) are people who claim they can detect water beneath the ground and, therefore, can advise you as to the best place to drill a well.

Talk to one or more dowsers. Generally, a well-drilling company will know who the local dowsers are. Ask a dowser to let you watch as he or she dowses. Try your hand at dowsing. Can you do it? Do you believe these people can really locate water with a divining rod? Most geologists and many well drillers are skeptical about dowsers. Talk to these people too.

If you believe dowsers are for real, see if you can find out how they do it. Does it require a certain skill? A certain body chemistry? Is it an ability that is inherited?

HOW MUCH AIR
DO YOU BREATHE?

When you breathe, air moves in and out of your lungs. The volume of air that you breathe can be measured with a spirometer; however, rough but reasonable measurements can be made with a plastic bag and a pail of water.

Calibrate a pail or large plastic container by pouring known volumes of water into the container and marking the water levels with a marking pen or a strip of narrow tape.

Pour a quart or two of water into the container so that the water level is on one of the lines you marked. Hold your nose so that all the air you breathe must pass through your mouth. When you have adjusted to mouth breathing, place the opening of a plastic bag (from which all the air has been removed) firmly around your mouth just before you exhale. Collect the exhaled air in the bag. (Do not blow; exhale in a normal way.) Twist the neck of the bag to seal off the exhaled air, and secure it with a tie band. **Caution: Never pull a plastic bag over your head.**

Then, holding the bag of air in your hand, push it under the water in the calibrated container. Mark the water level in the container before and after submerging the bag. Also mark your wrist at the water level. Finally, squeeze all the air out of the bag, hold it in your fist, and put your fist back into the water up to the mark on your wrist.

What is the volume of your hand and the empty bag? How can you find the volume of air that you exhaled? (This volume that you normally exhale is called your *tidal air* volume.)

Determine your breathing rate by counting the number of times you breathe in 1 min. Repeat this several times and take an average. From all your data, how much air do you breathe in one day?

Take the deepest breath you can and exhale as much air as possible into the plastic bag. This maximum volume of air that you can exhale is called your *vital capacity*. What is your vital capacity?

Compare the tidal air and vital capacities of a number of people. Are these volumes related to age? To gender? To height or weight? To chest size?

How about breathing rate? Is it related to age or sex? (Measure a baby's breathing rate.) Is it related to activity? How do sleep and exercise affect breathing rate?

Is tidal air affected by exercise? How about vital capacity? How about heart rate?

COKE VS. PEPSI

Can people really distinguish between Coke and Pepsi or between Coke and other brands of cola? Devise a taste test to find out. What do your results indicate?

Next, design a test to find out if things really do go better with Coke. Try some other comparisons:

- How about butter and margarine? Can people distinguish between the two? Can they distinguish butter from margarine when each substance is spread on bread?

- A number of different brands of bottled water or mineral water are sold in stores. Some people will buy only one brand because they think it is superior in taste to all the others. Can people really distinguish one brand of bottled water from the others? Do some tests to find out. Can subjects distinguish bottled water from tap water? Soft water from hard water?

- If possible, collect samples of tap water from various cities. Can people detect differences in the taste of these various city waters? If they can, which city has the best tasting water as determined by your taste test?

HOW DO YOU
LIKE YOUR EGGS,
BROWN OR WHITE?

In some parts of the country, white eggs cost more than brown eggs because people think white eggs taste better than brown eggs and are more nutritious. In other communities, brown eggs are more expensive for similar reasons.

Can people really distinguish between white eggs and brown eggs once they are cooked? Are brown eggs more nutritious?

Design some tests and experiments to answer these questions. If possible, have your results published in your local newspaper and see if you can affect the preferred egg color in a community where color is a factor in the pricing of eggs.

FASTER LEARNING

Design a series of exercises that will make younger students, including any younger brothers or sisters that you may have, better readers, listeners, observers, memorizers, or test takers. After doing your educational exercises, these students should be able to learn faster and more efficiently.

How can you test to see if your exercises are successful?

4
ANIMAL
SCIENCE

Animals are in themselves interesting subjects for scientific studies. Their behavior, adaptations, and mechanisms for reproduction and feeding are varied and fascinating. They are particularly of interest to researchers seeking to explain a variety of human behaviors and maladies.

If you choose one of these projects for a science fair, be sure to check the rules. Some fairs do not allow animal experiments. In any case, treat your animal subjects humanely.

TERRITORY

Animals often establish territories, areas they protect and regard as their own just as humans do, except that animals don't buy their territories with money—they establish them by aggressive and defensive behavior.

By watching the behavior of birds during their breeding season, you can locate their territories. Choose several acres of marsh or grassland. Make a map of the area so that you can locate and record the aggressive and defensive behavior, nest sites, and calls of each bird. Nesting and singing usually occur near the center of the bird's territory; aggressive actions are common at territorial edges.

See if you can determine the boundaries and areas of the territories you observe.

If you have dogs in your vicinity, see if you can find any evidence of territory among these animals.

Gypsy Moth Territory*

Before World War II, infestations by gypsy moths in the northeastern part of the United States occurred every 7 to 10 years. Since then, there appears to be no consistent pattern in the outbreaks. During the last outbreak, in 1981, the gypsy moths defoliated more than 12 million acres, turning vast areas of woodland from green to brown.

The best way to predict an infestation is to count egg masses on tree trunks in the fall and make rough predictions of how many will survive predators (spiders and beetles), parasites, disease, and climate.

Why has the previous 7- to 10-year pattern of gypsy moth infestation changed? How can we better predict a gypsy moth infestation? What can be done to prevent the extensive defoliation caused by these insects when their numbers become so large that natural predators and disease can no longer control their population?

A Nest in the Hand
Is Worth Studying

The fall or early winter is a good time to collect birds' nests. By then, most birds will have left their nests and many will have flown south. Most trees will be leafless, and grasses will have died, making nests easier to see. **Be careful in collecting nests; some may be**

high in trees. Get an adult to help you collect nests that are higher than you can reach from the ground. Keep in mind that certain birds may not return to a nest if people have touched it.

After recording where a nest was found and measuring its diameter, depth, and weight, use a field guide to identify the species of bird that made the nest. Or you may have seen the nest during the spring or summer and identified the birds that lived there. Remember, animals other than birds sometimes build in trees.

What materials do birds use to make their nests? Do different species use different materials, or do the differences lie solely in the way the nests are "woven" together and shaped?

Manmade materials such as string, plastic, and paper may be found in some nests. Do birds use these materials because they resemble natural materials from which they originally made nests? Or because manmade materials make better nests than the sticks, leaves, fur, and bark that were used before humans polluted the natural environment?

Which nests best protect eggs and offspring from predators? How are different nests designed to do this? How are nests fastened to trees? Do different species use different fastening techniques?

Which nests best resist weathering? Are these nests used by birds for more than one year? In the spring, place some nests back where you found them to see if any nests are used a second year.

Which nests have the strongest walls or bottoms? Is this related to the size of the bird that made the nest?

In the spring, place a variety of materials in your yard that you predict birds will and will not use to make nests. Then watch to see which items birds do use in making nests.

Which birds will live in birdhouses that you place in your yard? Are they the birds that build the weakest nests? Are they the same birds that use manmade birdbaths?

Finally, try to build a bird's nest. Why is it an easier task for birds than for you?

On the Snail Trail

Snails are nocturnal. They spend their days hidden away in cool, damp places under rock piles or pieces of wood and bark. Do snails return to the same daytime hideouts each morning?

To answer this question, you'll need about a dozen snails. Mark each snail's shell with small dots of fingernail polish or waterproof paint. Mark each snail so you can identify it, return it to its hiding place, and keep a record of where you found it.

Check the hideouts each morning to see if the snails return. If a snail fails to return, it may have been eaten by a predator or it may simply not return to the same place each day. To get meaningful data, try to mark as many snails as possible.

If, after two weeks, you find that snails do tend to return to the same place each morning, you can investigate how they find their way. Perhaps they use their eyes, which are located at the ends of the tentacles on the front ends of their bodies.

To find out if they see their way home, wait until a snail's tentacles are stretched way out. A snail will pull its tentacles back if it senses something is going to touch them. Slowly bring one of your fingers closer and closer to a snail's eye. At what point does a snail pull its tentacles back? Do you think a snail has good vision?

Maybe snails, like dogs, have a keen sense of smell. To find out, collect a few snails and put them in a container that is kept moist with a damp sponge.

Don't feed them for several days. Remove a snail and let it munch on a piece of lettuce or fruit for several minutes. Remove the food and place it a foot or two from the snail. Can the snail sniff its way to the food? How can you be sure it doesn't see the food?

Repeat the experiment with other snails. Do you think snails can smell their way home?

Watch a snail move slowly along the bottom of a container. You can see that it leaves a shiny mucus along its path. Perhaps the snail follows this mucus path back to its hideout every morning. Design experiments to test this hypothesis.

Can you think of other ways snails might find their way home? How can you test your hypotheses?

ANIMAL ACTIVITY

If you have mice, gerbils, or experimental rats, you can place an activity wheel in their cage and measure their activity by means of a counter that indicates the number of times the wheel turns. Are the animals more active during the day or at night?

Buy or borrow some other small animals. Are some species consistently more active than others? Do species vary in the time of day they are most active? Does the size or shape of the activity wheel have any effect on an animal's active time or the period of activity?

How Do Honey Bees Find Home?*
Studies have shown that honey bees use the sun to navigate. Have you ever found honey bees seeking nectar from flowers at night? Have you ever seen bees moving from flower to flower and back to their hive on a cloudy day? If so, how do they navigate? How do they find their way back to the hive?

[68]

Be careful making your observations. Honey bees can sting. Don't work with bees if you are allergic to bee stings. A beekeeper can provide you with protective equipment if necessary.

Ants Away from Home

Find an anthill and observe how ants come and go. Watch several ants. How far do they roam from their home? Remove an ant coming out of the hill, and put it at the maximum distance that you have observed an ant move from the hill. Can it find its way home? How do you think ants navigate? Design experiments to test your hypothesis.

Sweet and Sugar Sweet

Many people use saccharine or other artificial sweeteners in place of sugar. Some butterflies and other insects will feed on a solution of sugar. Design an experiment to see whether these insects distinguish between sugar and artificial sweeteners.

Cetology*

The study of whales is known as cetology. These mammals are the largest animals ever to live on Earth. Because they live in the sea, they are difficult to study and observe, but you can get fairly close to them by taking a journey on a whale-watching vessel. Scientists who study whales are called cetologists. These scientists often are associated with a whale-watching station along the Atlantic or Pacific coast. In addition to telling you that there is much we still do not know about these giant mammals, which have been hunted almost to extinction, a cetologist might appreciate your interest in whales and invite you to help him or her participate in one of the ongoing whale research programs.

Can you explain why whales sometimes swim

onto beaches and become stranded, or why they often leap out of the water (breach) and come crashing down onto the surface of the water? Sometimes they will repeat this behavior for as long as an hour. Many cetologists think this is a form of communication among whales. But *do* whales communicate? They certainly make sounds, both within their bodies and when they fall onto the sea or slam their flippers or tails on the water. Are these sounds a means of communication?

Whales also migrate over vast distances in the world's oceans. Whale watchers along both American coasts report that the same whales return year after year to the same waters. How do they navigate? Do they have built-in "compasses"? Or do they migrate by the stars and the sun?

Perhaps you can help a cetologist answer one of these questions.

Bird Migration*
Birds are much more visible and therefore easier to study than whales. During the fall and spring you can see flocks of migrating birds winging their way north or south. How do these birds know which way to fly? Do they navigate by the sun or the stars? Can they somehow use the earth's magnetic field to map their course? Perhaps you can begin to explain how birds find their way across continents and seas.

PREVENTING OR CURING THE COMMON COLD*

Some people claim that the common cold can be cured by drinking lemon and honey, eating chicken soup, or taking one of the over-the-counter cold remedies. Others maintain that the old adage still seems to hold: If you use a remedy, it will require seven days for the cold to disappear. If you do nothing, it will clear up in a week.

Dr. Linus Pauling, a Nobel Prize–winning chemist, believes that taking vitamin C will prevent people from catching colds. Other scientists disagree. Carry out your own investigations to decide for yourself whether vitamin C, lemon and honey, Dristan, or any of the other so-called cures or preventative methods actually work.

LIVING IN A MAGNETIC FIELD

As you may know, when electric charges move along a wire, there is an electric field within the wire pushing the charges. At the same time, another field, a magnetic field, surrounds the current. Some people claim that magnetic fields can have ill effects on living organisms. Are these claims valid? Are plants or animals living under power lines affected by the magnetic fields in which they live? Do people who live near power lines show a greater incidence of any abnormality?

You could do a more quantitative study in a laboratory setting. There you could vary the strength of the magnetic field in which the plants and animals live to see if there are any effects that do not appear in a control community of the same organisms. If effects are found, you can test to see how varying the field strength affects the results.

TOOTH DECAY AND SUGAR

You've probably been told that to prevent dental carries (cavities), you should brush after every meal and not eat between meals. The reason given is that sugars found in foods promote the growth of bacteria that cause tooth decay. By brushing and avoiding food between meals the concentration of sugars in the mouth is greatly reduced.

Do people who brush after every meal have fewer cavities? How about those who do not snack between meals? Does the amount of sugar in the diet affect the incidence of tooth decay?

You'll need a fairly large sample of young people to obtain enough data to answer these questions. Perhaps you can enlist the help of local dentists or obtain data from students in your school.

AGING: CAN IT BE PREVENTED?*

We all grow old, but must we? Doctors can replace worn-out knee and hip joints and transplant hearts, livers, and kidneys, but it would be better if these organs never wore out in the first place. Then replacements would not be necessary.

Are the cells of the elderly different from those of young people? What causes people to grow old? Can aging be prevented? Can you find the fountain of youth? Perhaps the way to start is to see if you can find out why mice and other animals with shorter life spans than humans grow old.

You may want to do a report-type project instead of an experimental one.

LONGER LIFE THROUGH BETTER EATING AND DRIVING

Many scientists believe that people would live longer if they were more careful about what they eat. Develop a diet designed to ensure a longer life through better eating habits.

Since strokes and heart attacks are two of the most common causes of death, your diet should certainly strive to reduce the incidence of these two killers.

Among younger people, accidental death, particularly from automobile collisions, is the most common cause of death. Diet alone cannot reduce this killer. See if you can develop a program that *will* reduce the high incidence of accidental death among young people.

THE HUMAN POPULATION

Recently, the world population was reported to be 5 billion people. But how do we know there are that many people in the world? How do governments go about the process of counting the people within their boundaries? Do the methods vary? Are some more accurate than others?

Could the world's population actually be 6 billion? Or 4 billion? How accurately do we know the world's human population?

If the count is accurate, are we the most numerous mammal on earth? What species of animals exceed the human population?

5

PLANT

SCIENCE

f you have a "green thumb," there are some projects in this chapter that you will want to try. You may even want to use one or more of the projects in science fairs. But not all plants are green. Some nongreen plants are responsible for making nitrogen available to other plants and for maintaining the natural cycles that convert dead organic matter into the chemicals that can be used again by living organisms.

TURNING WHITE FLOWERS
RED, GREEN, AND BLUE

During the summer in many parts of the world, Queen Anne's lace can be found blooming in fields and along highways. Its clusters of tiny flowers have white petals. You can turn the white flowers to blue, red, or green quite easily. Cut a few stalks of Queen Anne's lace when the flower is in bloom. Place one or two stalks in separate containers of water. To each container add a different food coloring. After several hours you will see the petals turn color. Does the depth of color increase with time? If Queen Anne's lace is in bloom on the 4th of July, you could make a red, white, and blue bouquet.

How does the color get into the flowers? Can you produce purple flowers by mixing red and blue food coloring in a container? In how many different colors can you "paint" the petals?

Will this method of changing the color of flowers work for other flowers that have white petals? Will yellow flowers turn green if placed in blue water?

LEAF IMAGES

Without light, green plants cannot produce the chlorophyll that gives them their characteristic color. You can use this fact to make images on the surface of green leaves. Use scissors to cut a particular shape or pattern from the center of a small piece of aluminum foil. Attach the foil firmly to a large geranium leaf with paper clips as shown in Figure 11. Be sure there is no space between the leaf and the aluminum.

Place the plant in bright sunlight. After a week, gently remove the foil from the leaf. You should see an image on the leaf "film." What happens to the leaf "print" after it is exposed to sunlight for some time? What happens if you cover the leaf with a photographic negative instead of aluminum foil?

OTHER COLORED GRASS*

Grass is green because it contains the pigment chlorophyll. Leaves contain chlorophyll and other pigments such as xanthophyll, which is yellow, and the yellowish-orange pigment carotene. Like colors in autumn leaves, they appear only when the concentration of chlorophyll is diminished to the point where these less abundant colored pigments become visible.

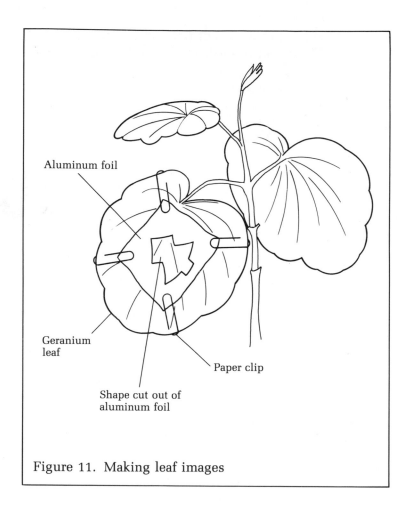

Aluminum foil

Geranium leaf

Paper clip

Shape cut out of aluminum foil

Figure 11. Making leaf images

Can you find a way to grow a grass that is orange or yellow instead of green? With your parents' permission, you might even grow your initials on your lawn.

WHERE ARE THE LEAVES LARGEST?

Look closely at the leaves on a variety of trees. Do you notice any relationship between the size of the leaves and their position on the tree? Do leaves near the top of the tree tend to be smaller than those near the base? Do leaves become smaller the farther out on a limb they are located?

FIRST SITES OF AUTUMN COLORS

As summer heat begins to fade and the brilliant colors of autumn become imminent, watch to see where the first leaves with patches of red, orange, and yellow colors appear. Do these colored leaves appear first on one type of tree such as maples? Do the trees where these colors first appear have anything in common? For example, are they close to the roadside where salt concentrations may be greater due to winter "sandings," or on the south side of trees where the sunlight is more intense and longer lasting?

If you think you have an explanation as to why the first colors of autumn appear in particular places, design ways to test your explanation.

LONG- AND SHORT-DAY PLANTS

Flowers bloom at different times of the year. Could the amount of sunlight they receive determine their blooming season?

To find out, buy some cosmos or dill seeds and some petunia or marigold seeds. About midway through May, plant twenty-five cosmos or dill seeds in each of two large, soil-filled pots. Follow the directions for planting on the package. Plant twenty-five petunia or marigold seeds in each of two other pots. Label the pots and be sure to water all the seeds every few days. The soil should be kept moist but not wet. Don't drown the seeds.

[77]

When the plants are about 2 in (5 cm) tall, pull out any that are very tall or short, leaving about ten in each pot that are nearly the same size. Put the pots in a place where they will receive as much sunlight as possible.

When the plants are about four weeks old, cover one of the pots that contain dill or cosmos plants and one of the pots containing petunias or marigolds so that they both receive about 9 h of light each day instead of the 15 h characteristic of a normal early summer day. Leave the other two pots as controls; that is, let these plants receive the normal 15 h of light each day. In this way, you can see the effect of a shorter day on the experimental plants, which will be the only difference between the two sets of plants. Use cardboard boxes large enough to cover pots and plants completely. To ensure that light doesn't penetrate the box, seal all edges and seams with black tape. The experimental plants should be exposed to light from about 8 A.M. until 5 P.M. The controls should get all the sunlight that a normal long summer day can offer. Continue the experiment until each species of plant has bloomed.

Does the amount of sunlight a plant receives affect its blooming? What evidence do you have? How do other plants respond to the length of day? If you repeat this experiment in the winter using artificial light, do you get similar results?

STOMATE DENSITY

The surface of a leaf has many small openings called *stomates* that allow gases to move in and out of leaf tissue. To see some stomates, fold a geranium leaf and remove a small section of the lower epidermis with forceps. Add the tissue to a drop of water on a microscope slide and cover with a glass cover slip. Through a microscope you will see that the openings are surrounded by bean-shaped *guard cells*. How do you think these guard cells surrounding the stomates control the movement of moisture within the plant? What can you do to test your idea?

How many stomates do you see in your field of view under the microscope? Examine other sections of the same leaf tissue with the microscope. What is the average number of stomates per visible area? Estimate the approximate number of stomates on a geranium leaf. On the entire plant. On the leaves of an average-size maple tree.

Is the density of stomates on the leaves of other plants comparable to that of a geranium? If not, can you find factors that determine stomate density (number per area)?

COLORED MULCH

Many gardeners put mulch around plants to reduce loss of moisture and inhibit weed growth. Some use black or other opaque plastic for similar reasons. Recent studies at Clemson University suggest that the color of the plastic placed around the plants affects their growth. For example, preliminary studies show that tomatoes grown over red plastic produced larger and greater numbers of fruit than control plants.

Try experiments of your own to see how, or if, tomatoes and other plants are affected by the color of the light reflected onto the plant. Or is it a color effect? Might not the temperature of the soil warmed by the plastic covering be the primary factor here?

THE INS AND OUTS OF PLANT CELLS

Plant cells are surrounded by thick cell walls. Inside the wall is a thin *semipermeable* membrane that surrounds the cytoplasm. The membrane is called semipermeable because it allows some substances, such as water, to pass through it but prevents the passage of other substances, such as starch. Near the center of a plant cell is a *vacuole* that also is surrounded by a semipermeable membrane. When water fills the vacuoles, the cells and, hence, the plant tissues are plump and firm. If water leaves the vacuoles, the plant becomes limp and appears wilted.

To see what happens when water moves into or out of a large number of plant cells, use an apple corer or cork borer to remove long cylinders of root tissue from a rutabaga. Cut each cylinder into sections about 1/2 in (13 mm) long. Prepare about fifty pieces and divide them into five groups of ten. Find the mass of each group and record your data.

Put the first group of rutabaga disks into a cup of water, the second into a cup of water in which 1/2 teaspoon of salt has been dissolved. Place the third, fourth, and fifth sets in cups of water to which 1, 2, and 3 teaspoons of salt have been dissolved, respectively. After an hour, remove the rutabaga from each liquid and blot the tissue dry with paper towels.

Which groups of disks feel firm? Which feel limp? Can you predict which groups have added water to their cells? Which have lost water? To test your predictions, weigh each set of rutabaga again. What do you find? Were your predictions correct?

Beets are red because their cell vacuoles contain a substance that has a red color. If the semipermeable membranes surrounding the vacuoles are destroyed, the red color will leak out of the cells.

To see this effect, peel a beet and cut it into about one hundred cubes 1/2 in (13mm) on a side. Put the cubes in a pan of cold water. After 10 min, pour off the water. Rinse the beet cubes until no more red color appears so you can be sure that the contents of all injured cells have been removed.

Place a dozen beet cubes in each of eight containers. To five of the containers add a cup of the same liquids you used with the rutabaga. To one of the other three containers add a cup of boiling water. To another add a cup of 50% water and 50% rubbing alcohol. To the last add a cup of rubbing alcohol. Watch for the appearance of a red color in the liquids during the next half hour.

Can you predict which liquids will destroy the semipermeable membranes? How can you tell if you are right? Can you modify this experiment so as to actually see the effect of these liquids on the cells?

ARE STUNTED, POT-BOUND PLANTS MORE PRODUCTIVE?

Some botanists claim that a plant grown in a pot that is too small will restrict root growth and stunt the growing plant. Others claim that while small pots restrict the growth of plants, the reduced space occupied by such plants allows for a greater production of fruit (tomatoes, for example) per unit space than plants grown in larger pots.

Design experiments of your own to see if pot-bound plants are more efficient fruit producers in terms of space. Do your results apply to most kinds of plants?

FINDING BACTERIA

This experiment should be done under the supervision of a knowledgeable science teacher or biologist. Some bacteria can cause disease.

You can't see bacterial cells without a microscope, but if a large number are present, you can see the cluster they form. To produce a cluster of bacteria big enough to see, you need to collect a small number of bacteria and provide them with food.

Since many common bacteria will grow on potatoes, cut slices ¼ in (6mm) thick from peeled potatoes and place each slice on a petri dish or jar cap. Add a teaspoon of water and cover each petri dish or lid with a larger dish or lid. Next, put about twenty-five toothpicks and cotton swabs in a can and cover it with aluminum foil. Place the can and dishes or lids on a pan. Put the pan into the oven and heat at 250°F (120°C) for about an hour. This should sterilize everything on the pan.

Once the materials have cooled, you'll be ready to start collecting bacteria. Carefully lift one side of the top from the can of toothpicks or cotton swabs. Remove one of the toothpicks and quickly replace the cover so that bacteria in the air cannot fall into the can. Scrape the inside of your cheek with the toothpick. Then lift one side of a lid or petri dish cover and spread the material on the end of the toothpick over the surface of the potato slice. Replace the cover.

In a similar manner, using toothpicks or cotton swabs, collect samples from under your fingernails, on your skin, and from soil, floors, or other places where you think bacteria may be found. Expose a few potato slices to the air for about 10 min in different locations to see if bacteria will collect on the potato. You might try such places as a kitchen, basement, windowsill, sidewalk, and refrigerator.

Leave one or more sterilized potato slices untouched to serve as a control. If nothing grows on these potatoes, you can be quite sure the other potato slices were sterile before they were touched.

Label each jar lid or petri dish. Record the name of the substance you added to the potato and the date you did it. Put the potato slices in their containers in a warm place, up to about 100°F (38°C), where they will not be disturbed. Examine the bacteria daily **as directed by your adult supervisor.** A colony of bacteria will appear as a spot on the potato. Which of the substances tested seem to have held bacteria?

When you've finished the experiment, discard the bacteria **as directed by your adult supervisor.**

Design an experiment to see how temperature affects the growth of bacteria. Obtain approval from your adult supervisor before carrying out your experiment.

Does washing your hands really kill bacteria? Do antiseptics and detergents deter the growth of bacteria? How can you find out?

DO PLANTS HAVE "EARS"?

Many plant lovers believe that plants grow better if you talk to them. You probably don't want to spend your day talking to a plant, but you can play music in the vicinity of plants and see if it affects their growth.

You'll need a set of control plant seedlings placed in a quiet place away from noise. Comparable sets of experimental plant seedlings can be placed in similar conditions as far as light, moisture, and soil are concerned, but these plants should be subjected to various types of music. For example, one set might "listen" to classical music while rock music is played for another set of plants.

Does music affect the growth of plants? Do plants respond better to one particular type of music?

THE ASCENT
OF SAP IN TREES*

The pressure exerted by the atmosphere at sea level can support a column of water about 34 ft (10 m) high.

Since sap rises in some tall trees to heights as great as 300 ft (90 m), air pressure cannot explain the ascent of sap even if there were a perfect vacuum at the tops of such trees, which isn't the case.

How then can sap ascend to such large heights in trees? What is the source of the pressure or force that makes this possible?

THE LIFE AND DEATH
OF A YEAST CULTURE

Prepare a yeast culture by mixing bread yeast that you can buy at a grocery store with water as directed on the package. Place a drop or two in about 15 mL of a saturated sugar solution in a test tube. Cork and shake the tube gently.

To determine the population of the culture, place a drop from the center of the culture on a microscope slide, add a cover slip, and count the number of yeast visible in each of several views under a microscope. Repeat the sampling technique at 1-h intervals for at least 12 h. Continue your count the next morning and longer if possible. You may have to dilute the sample to make an accurate count.

Plot a graph of the yeast population as a function of time. What can you conclude? Is the graph affected when the yeast are grown at different temperatures?

To make your task easier, you might use a computer interfaced with a light-sensitive probe. The amount of light passing through the test tube will diminish as the population of yeast grows. Prepared computer programs will enable you to plot the yeast population on the computer, or you can write your own program for doing this.

Once you've found a way to use the computer to make the task of measuring yeast populations easier, you might like to look at the effect of the initial sugar concentration, the kind of yeast, and the type of sugar (sucrose, lactose, or maltose), as well as different colored light on the population curve. With a pH probe you could test the carbon dioxide production of the culture as a function of time and population, as well.

6

PHYSICS AND ENGINEERING

The fundamental laws of physics, established primarily by Sir Isaac Newton in the 17th century, have served as a foundation for understanding the natural world and for developing a technology that has changed the way we travel, communicate, and live. Since Newton's time, there have been modifications of these basic laws, and atomic physicists have extended them to the very small dimensions of the atomic nucleus, where new forces were discovered. Astronomers have extended the same laws to the edges of the universe, where discoveries have led to the notion of black holes and other ideas never dreamed of by Newton.

MEASURING SPEEDS AND VELOCITIES

Speed and velocity do not have the same meaning. Speed is a measurement of how far something travels in a certain time. The speedometer on a car measures speed. But a car's velocity includes the direction it is moving as well as its speed. If you say a car is going northwest at 50 mph, you have reported its velocity.

The projects that follow all involve measurements of speed or velocity.

Strobing or Filming

Use a stroboscope and camera, a high-speed motion picture camera, or a computer to measure the speed and velocity of a falling object, a pitched baseball, an accelerating cart, cars on a highway, sprinters on a track, and other fast-moving objects. **(Be sure you are in a safe position before filming.)** In which cases is the speed relatively constant? In which cases does speed or velocity change with time? Try to account for accelerations (changes in velocity).

Speeding Athletes and Animals

Use whatever method seems best to compare the speeds of various athletes in action. Is hockey really the fastest team sport? Is the speed of a runner related to the distance of the event in which he or she runs? How does the speed of a javelin compare with the speed of the athlete who launched it?

It may be quite easy to measure the speed of a racing horse or greyhound, and you may find it relatively simple to measure the speed of your own pet, but to find the speed of wild animals you may have to use movies made by others. How can you use such films to estimate the speed of various animals?

Estimating Speeds

On a highway, you may wonder how fast another car is traveling when it passes you. Find a way to estimate the speed of cars that pass you. Can you also find a way to estimate the speed of cars approaching you?

What about airplanes? Can you estimate their speeds? Here, of course, it's important to know how far away the plane is. A nearby Piper Cub that is landing may appear to be moving much faster than a jet 5 mi (8 km) overhead.

THE SPEED OF
SOUND IN AIR

At a baseball game, you see a batter hit the ball before you hear the sound caused by the collision of bat and ball. The fact that light travels about a million times faster than sound provides the most direct method for measuring the speed of sound in air.

Have someone who is far away (about half a mile or 800 m) make a loud sound by doing something that you can see, such as hitting a board with a hammer. Start a stopwatch at the moment you see the hammer strike the board. Stop the watch when you hear the sound. Knowing the distance and the time, you can calculate the speed of sound.

■ A more sophisticated method of measuring the speed of sound involves the principle of resonance, which occurs when a piano string, or any other object that has the same natural vibration frequency, vibrates when the same note is played on another instrument.

Air in organ pipes and flutes, as well as in soda bottles, also emit sounds by resonating. Hold a vibrating tuning fork over a tall, air-filled cylinder. By adding water to the cylinder, you can change the length of the air column until its resonant frequency matches that of the tuning fork. When the frequencies match, the sound will be loudest.

You can show that for a tube open at one end, resonance first occurs when the length of the air column is one-fourth the length of the sound's wavelength.

[88]

To measure the wavelength, nearly fill a tall cylindrical jar with water. Place a narrower tube, open at both ends and about 20 in (50 cm) long, into the jar of water, as shown in Figure 12. You can vary the length of the air column above the water in the narrower tube by moving the tube up or down.

Set a tuning fork with a frequency of about 200 to 300 Hz into vibration. Hold the fork horizontally, its tines one above the other, just above the open end of the tube. Move fork and tube up and down until the air column length emits the loudest sound. Measure the length of this air column. Since it is one-fourth the wavelength of the sound, what is the wavelength of the sound resonating in the tube?

From the wavelength and the frequency, determine the speed of sound. Repeat the experiment using a different tuning fork. Is the wavelength the same as before? Is the speed of sound still the same?

■ The speed of sound can also be measured with an oscilloscope, an audio oscillator, and a microphone. The setup is shown in Figure 13. The audio oscillator is connected to the speaker and to the horizontal input terminals of an oscilloscope. The microphone is connected to the vertical input terminals of the scope.

After setting the oscilloscope for an external sweep operation, set the audio oscillator for about 500 Hz. Increase the gain on the oscilloscope until you can hear a tone. Move apart the wooden supports on which the oscillator and microphone rest. As the distance between oscillator and microphone increases, you'll see Lissajous patterns (diagonal lines when the horizontal and vertical signals are in phase or

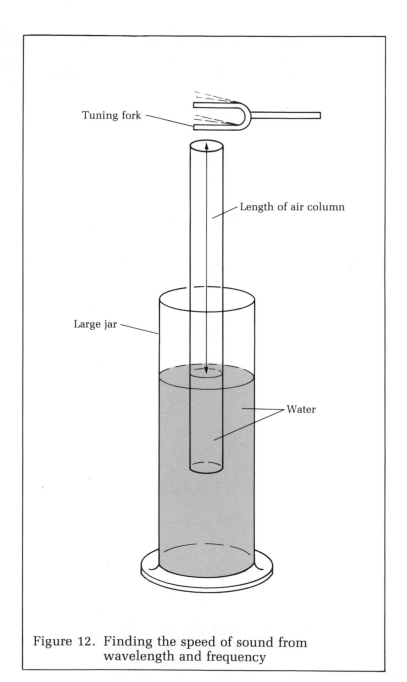

Figure 12. Finding the speed of sound from wavelength and frequency

180 degrees out of phase and ovals and circles otherwise) on the scope face. Each time the pattern changes by one wavelength, the Lissajous pattern will change by 360 degrees, or from one straight line to another straight line.

By measuring the change in distance between the sound source and the microphone required for a full 360-degree change, you can determine the wavelength of the audio frequency used. From the product of the wavelength and the frequency, you can calculate the speed of the sound.

Explain why a change of 360 degrees in the Lissajous pattern indicates a change of one wavelength in the phase.

■ A more direct method of measuring the speed of sound can be found in an article entitled "High Precision Method of Measuring the Velocity of Sound with Simple Apparatus" that appeared in the February 1975 issue of *The Physics Teacher.*

■ Standing-wave patterns made by two point sources of sound that set up an interference pattern, similar to Young's experiment for measuring the wavelength of light (see page 00), can also be used to measure the wavelength of a sound of known frequency. (See Figure 13, B and C.)

Which of the methods you used to measure the speed of sound is the most accurate?

■ Does temperature affect the speed of sound? Design an experiment to find out. Then explain your results if you can.

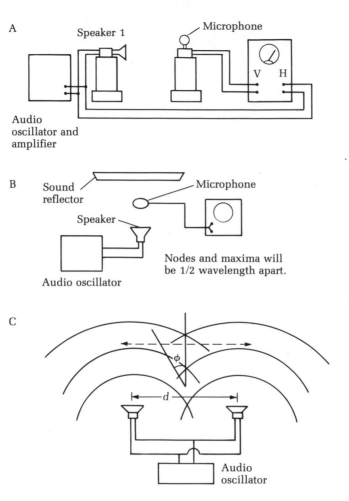

A   Speaker 1   Microphone

Audio
oscillator and
amplifier

B   Sound   Microphone
     reflector

     Speaker

                        Nodes and maxima will
                        be 1/2 wavelength apart.
     Audio oscillator

C

                        ϕ

                        d

                        Audio
                        oscillator

Outside, on a calm day, set up line perpendicular to d along
central maximum. Move ear along line perpendicular to
central max to find other maxima or nodes. From geometry
of interference pattern:

$$\lambda = \frac{dx}{nL}$$

Figure 13. Measuring the speed of sound using
            electronics

THE SPEED OF SOUND
AND AIR PRESSURE

It can be shown theoretically that the speed of sound should not be affected by air pressure, because the density of a gas is proportional to its pressure. Can you devise an experimental means of testing this theory?

THE SPEED OF TV WAVES

The frequency of the electromagnetic waves broadcast by a television station is announced at sign-off time and when the station begins broadcasting in the morning. If you know the wavelength of the waves generated by the station's transmitting antenna, you can determine the speed of the waves in air because the velocity of the waves must equal the product of the wavelength and the frequency.

To find the wavelength of the TV waves, place a TV set between you and the antenna of the station to which you are tuned. A phone call to the station will enable you to find the location of the transmitting antenna. (Often the station is not at the same location as the antenna.)

Turn the TV so you can see the picture. Then turn the receiving antenna on the set so that it lies in a plane perpendicular to a line connecting the transmitting and receiving antennas. Use the fine-tuning control to "detune" the set so that the reception is not very good.

With a large sheet of aluminum foil taped to a sheet of cardboard, you can create an interference pattern that will cause the picture to alternately blur and clear up. Keeping the aluminum reflector parallel to the receiving antenna (perpendicular to the line connecting set and transmitting antenna), move the sheet toward and away from the receiving antenna. Record the distances between successive losses of picture

[93]

reception as you move the reflector away from the set. Since the waves undergo a phase shift of 180 degrees upon reflection, the distance D from set to aluminum reflector is given by

$$D = nW/2,$$

where n is an integer and W is the wavelength.

What is the wavelength of the TV waves from this station? What is the speed of these electromagnetic waves? How does this compare with the speed of light? Design an experiment to determine the speed of light from distance and time measurements.

For more information, see "Estimating the Speed of Light with a TV Set" in the September 1985 issue of *The Physics Teacher*.

PROJECTING PROJECTILES

Knowing all that you do about gravity, acceleration, velocity, momentum, and kinetic energy, you can hold a contest to determine who can throw a baseball highest and fastest.

Have a contestant throw a ball straight up into the air. At the moment the ball leaves the thrower's hand, start a stopwatch. Stop the watch when the ball is caught. From the time recorded on the watch, calculate the height to which the ball ascended. Who can throw the ball highest? Highest is also fastest in this case. Why?

To see who can throw a ball fastest in a horizontal direction, have contestants throw from an elevated height, such as the top of a hill or some bleachers. The time the ball is in the air after it leaves the thrower's hand and the distance it travels horizontally should enable you to determine the speed with which the ball was thrown.

Finally, have contestants throw a ball as far as they can from a fixed line, such as the goal line on a football field. Use the time of flight and the horizontal distance traveled by the ball to calculate the maximum height the ball rose, the velocity of the ball as it left the thrower's hand, and the angle the ball was thrown upward relative to the horizon. What additional information do you need to determine the average force that the thrower exerted on the ball?

Will the type of ball thrown have any effect on the speed, height, and distance that the ball will travel? On the average force with which it is thrown?

JUDGING FLY BALLS*

One of the most difficult feats in baseball is judging a fly ball. Somehow a good outfielder learns to move in the right direction as soon as a ball is hit. But if you ask outfielders how they know which way to move, chances are they won't be able to tell you. However, many will tell you that the most difficult balls to judge are ones that are hit directly at them. This would suggest that being able to see the initial angle the ball is traveling when it leaves the bat is a clue to proper judgment.

Make an investigation of this difficult but learnable feat and see if you can figure out how it is done. It may be helpful to work with both a novice and an experienced fielder.

SAILING INTO THE WIND

Experienced sailors know that you can sail into the wind by tacking, that is, by angling back and forth in zigzag fashion. In fact, a sailboat can exceed wind speed while tacking, but its maximum speed while sailing downwind is the speed of the wind.

See if you can explain these rather strange facts of sailing. Building a "sailboat" like the one in Figure 14 and propelling it with wind from a fan may help you in solving this perplexing problem.

Before you start, you should understand that the direction of the force on a sail is always perpendicular to the sail's surface. If the force was not perpendicular to the sail, there would have to be a component of the force parallel to the sail's surface. Such a force would have nothing to push against and, therefore, cannot exist. Of course, the sailboat does not have to move in the direction of the force on the sail because a keel keeps it moving in the direction of the bow.

A SETTLING QUESTION

When you first open a box of cornflakes, or some other flaky cereal, the large crispy flakes lie there at the top tempting your palate. By the time you reach the bottom of the box, the flakes have shrunk to the size of dust particles.

Why is it that the large flakes seem to "settle" to the top? One way to begin this project might be to see if the same thing occurs when you mix stones of different sizes and shake them in a closed container.

ROLLING AND SLIDING
ON BREADBOARD HILL

Find a toy car or truck of good size with wheels that turn freely. Place the car on a board. How high do you have to raise one end of the board to make the car roll? What is the frictional force between the car and the board?

Place a wide rubber band around both the front and rear wheels so that the wheels cannot turn. The rubber bands act as brakes on the wheels. How high

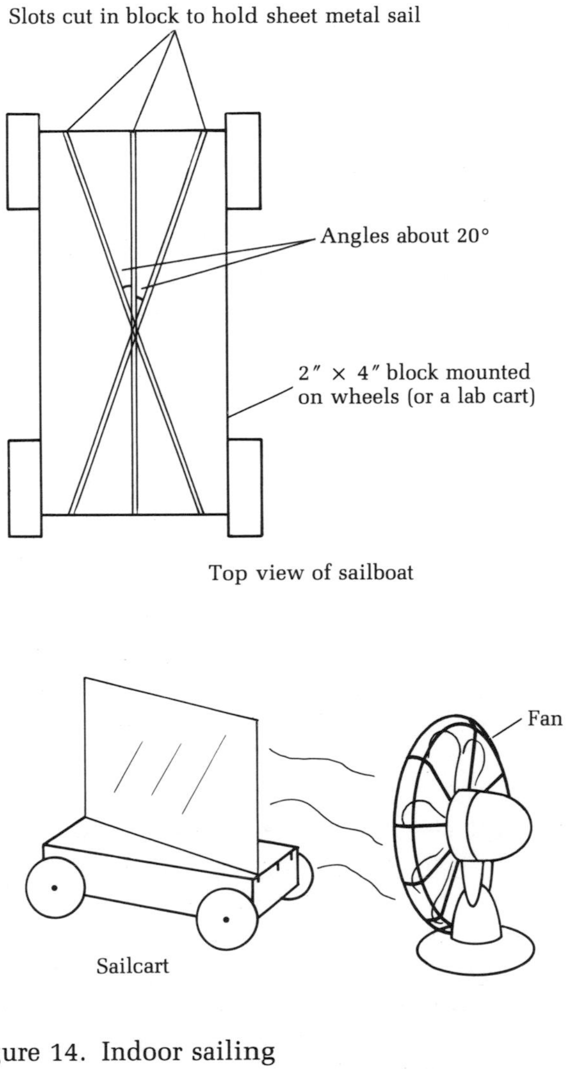

Slots cut in block to hold sheet metal sail

Angles about 20°

2″ × 4″ block mounted
on wheels (or a lab cart)

Top view of sailboat

Fan

Sailcart

Figure 14. Indoor sailing

do you have to raise the board to make the car move now? What has happened to the frictional force between the car and the board?

Remove the rubber band from the front wheels so that only the rear wheels are braked. Again raise the board. What happens this time? What happens when you raise the board with the front wheels locked in the brake position and the rear wheels free to turn?

Explain why braking only the front wheels has a different effect than braking only the rear wheels. Which brakes on a car "grab" first? (You can find out by watching from a **safe distance** as slowly moving cars brake on a slippery incline.) Explain why cars are made to brake this way.

ELECTRICAL RESISTANCE IN A PLATING CELL

You probably know that the electrical resistance of a wire depends on its length, diameter, temperature, and composition, but what variables affect the resistance of a plating cell such as the copper plating cell shown in Figure 15.

To find out, prepare a 1-M solution of copper sulfate by dissolving 250 g of copper sulfate crystals ($CuSO_4 \cdot 5H_2O$) in enough distilled water to make 1L of solution.

Pour about 200 mL of the solution into a 250-mL beaker. Fasten sheet copper or copper mesh electrodes securely at opposite sides of the beaker. Connect a power source to the plating cell so that you can establish a current of about 1.0 A through the solution. Using an ammeter and a voltmeter, connected as shown in the drawing, you can determine the resistance across the cell.

The ratio of the potential difference (voltage) across the cell to the current through the cell measures the cell's resistance. The resistance of most metal

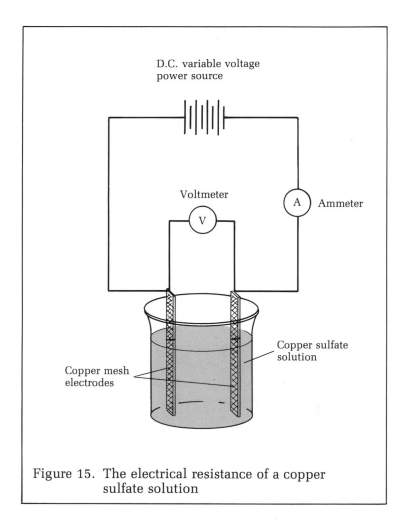

Figure 15. The electrical resistance of a copper
        sulfate solution

wires increases with temperature. Is the resistance of
a copper plating cell related in any way to the temperature of the solution? Does the temperature of the
solution change as current flows through the cell? If it
does, what can you do to prevent the temperature
from changing while other variables are tested?

    How is the resistance of the copper plating cell
related to the distance between the electrodes? Is the

resistance of the cell affected by the area of the electrodes?

You can change the concentration of the solution used in the cell by diluting a sample of the 1-M solution you prepared. For example, adding 100 mL of distilled water to an equal volume of the 1-M solution will give 200 mL of a 0.50-M solution. How would you prepare solutions that are 0.80 M, 0.60 M, 0.40 M, 0.20 M, and 0.1 M? Does the concentration of the solution affect the resistance of the cell?

TEMPERATURE AND SHELF LIFE

Many people keep D-cells and other electric cells or batteries in the refrigerator. They claim the cells will last longer (have a longer shelf life) if they are kept cool.

Design an experiment to see if electric cells, such as D- or C-cells, do last longer if kept cool.

If you find that shelf life is increased by storing the cells at low temperatures, would a freezer be better than a refrigerator for storing these cells?

MAKE A SUPERCONDUCTING MATERIAL*

At very low temperatures some materials become superconductors; that is, the electrical resistance of the material becomes zero. With ordinary conductors, energy, in the form of thermal energy, is released at a rate equal to V^2/R or I^2R along conductors. (V represents the potential difference, or voltage, across the conductor, I is the current, and R is the resistance of the conductor.) With superconductors, no thermal energy arises from current flow through a potential difference. All the electrical energy can be used to do useful work.

Until recently, materials had to be lowered to temperatures very close to the coldest temperature possible, a chilly −460°F (−273°C) before they became superconductors. This required expensive coolants such as liquid helium. But during the past several years, scientists at IBM's Almaden Research Center and elsewhere have discovered materials that become superconductors at temperatures higher than −319°F (−195°C).

Since liquid nitrogen, which is a relatively inexpensive and abundant coolant, has a boiling point of −319°F, the use of superconductors on a much wider scale has become an economic possibility. Of course, much work remains to be done because the materials that become superconductors at such relatively high temperatures must be made in a form that is a practical means of transporting electric current.

One material that becomes a superconductor at the temperature of liquid nitrogen is the ceramic $YBa_2Cu_3O_7$. David Pribyl, a Gilroy, California, science teacher, has developed a process for making this ceramic based on a technique used by Paul Grant and his colleagues at the Almaden Research Center. You can obtain a copy of this technique by writing to David Pribyl, Science Department, Gilroy High School, Gilroy, CA 95020. Include a stamped, self-addressed envelope.

For additional information on projects involving superconductivity see the following articles:

"Superconductors: Better Levitation through Chemistry," and "Levitating a Magnet Using a Superconductive Material," *Journal of Chemical Education*, October, 1987, pp 836 and 851.

To obtain a kit of materials needed to demonstrate superconductivity write to:

Institute for Chemical Education
Project 1-2-3
Department of Chemistry
University of Wisconsin-Madison
Madison, WI 53706

A BICYCLE
POWER STATION

Electrical power in this country is most often produced from steam generated by burning oil, coal, or
natural gas, or by the fission of uranium or plutonium.
It is also generated in smaller quantities from hydro-
power, geothermal energy, windmills, and solar energy. Now, you can add yet another method of producing electricity—bike power.

Find a way to connect your bicycle to an automobile generator so that when you pedal, the generator
produces electricity. How much power, in kilowatts,
can you develop? How long can you sustain your maximum power output?

You can also use this device to measure the power
output of different people. Who is the most powerful
human you can find and test?

THE PHYSICS OF SCALING

In Jonathan Swift's book *Gulliver's Travels*, Lemuel
Gulliver visited a kingdom called Lilliput, where all
living things were built on a scale of 1 in to the foot, a
ratio of 1:12. Lilliputians were about 6 in tall with
waists a little less than 3 in in circumference. Gulliver
also visited a land of giants—Brobdingnag—where
humans and other living creatures were 12 times as
large as we are. A Brobdingnagian was about 70 ft tall
and weighed nearly a ton.

Long before Swift wrote this satire, Galileo had

explained why people as large as Brobdingnagians or as small as Lilliputians could never exist. The physics of scaling forbids insects as large as dinosaurs or humans as large as King Kong. In the words of Galileo,

> If one wishes to maintain in a great giant the same proportion of limb as that found in an ordinary man he must either use a harder and stronger material for making the bones, or he must admit a diminution of strength in comparison with men of medium stature; for if his height be increased inordinately he will fall and be crushed under his own weight. Whereas, if the size of a body be diminished, the strength of that body is not diminished in the same proportion; indeed, the smaller the body, the greater its relative strength. Thus a small dog could probably carry on his back two or three dogs of his own size; but I believe a horse could not carry even one of his own size.

Expand on Galileo's argument to show why organisms cannot be scaled up or down by a factor of 10. Think about how strength is related to the cross-sectional area of bone; how weight varies with a scale factor that applies in all dimensions—width and length as well as height; and how food requirements and heat loss, which involve body weight and surface area, respectively, are related to the scale factor.

You may find it useful to work with clay as you build scale models of some basic form. For example, a cube could represent a body; small cylinders could represent the legs used to support the body.

After you've completed your project, you should understand why an elephant's legs are so thick, why beached whales and wet insects generally are doomed, why there are no warm-blooded animals as small as a fly, and why small animals are seldom found in polar regions.

SOLVING THE FRUSTRATION OF A LOCKED CAR

Nothing is more frustrating to a driver than to find that the keys to his or her car are locked inside the car. Bent coat hangers, a call for a police officer, or an emergency call to a garage may solve the problem, but it's a slow process.

See if you can invent a way that will enable drivers to open their car, and only their car, if the keys are accidentally locked inside.

INVENT A SPRINGY CAR

Thousands of people are killed each year in automobile accidents. Often the victims are crushed or trapped inside because the car's body collapses during these inelastic collisions. Perhaps you can build a safer car and reduce the incidence of death on the highway. Couldn't cars be made of springy materials that would convert the kinetic energy going into the collision into elastic potential energy? Might not these more elastic collisions reduce highway death and injury?

Would a truly wraparound bumper made of elastic material make cars safer? Would such a car be too expensive? Couldn't costs be reduced by incorporating the elastic material into the car's basic structure?

You may want to start with scale models of your designs for safer cars. If your models prove successful, Ford, GMC, Chrysler, Honda, or some other car manufacturer may finance your research so that you can build full-size safe cars.

CARS ON CURVES

When a car moves along a circular path, the outside wheel must go farther and, therefore, turn around more times than the inside wheel. The differential gear in a car allows one wheel to turn faster than the other while power is supplied to the axle through the drive shaft.

How do trains allow for the difference in wheel speed as they round a curve?

Can you design an alternative to the differential for getting automobiles around curves?

JETS ON THE HIGHWAY?

Jet engines power many commercial, private, and military airplanes, but we don't find jet-powered automobiles on highways. Why not? Would they be too fast to be safe? Or are they too expensive to build?

See if you can find the answer to this question. You might want to build a jet-powered model car if you think it's feasible.

TIPPY CANOES

If you've ever paddled a canoe, you know it's much less stable than a rowboat. That's why you've probably been told never to stand up in a canoe. But why are canoes so unstable? And if they're so tippy, why do people use them?

Design a canoe that is safer and still retains the properties that make these boats popular.

GO FLY A KITE

Benjamin Franklin used a kite to investigate electricity, but don't you try it—it's very dangerous. Franklin

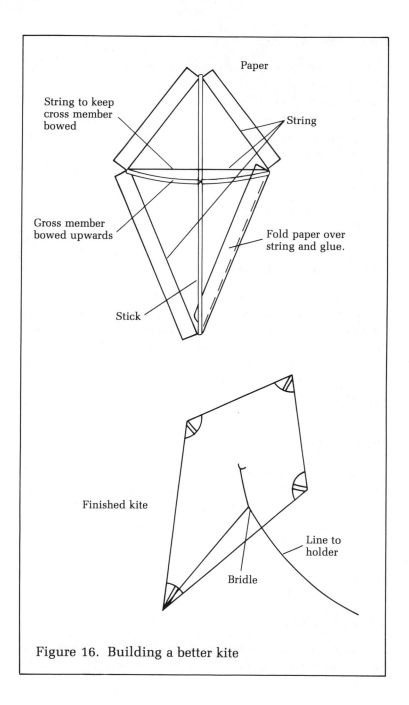

Figure 16. Building a better kite

was lucky he wasn't killed while flying a kite in a thunderstorm. The Chinese used kites in celebrations thousands of years ago, and that's a safer use as long as you stay in open fields away from power lines and lightning.

You can build a kite from sticks of lightweight wood, string, glue, and lightweight paper. (My grandfather used newspaper.) If you think your kite needs a tail, you can tie together pieces of old cloth.

The frame of the kite is made from sticks and string, as shown in Figure 16. Grandpa notched the sticks so that the string would stay in place. He said that a kite should be 1½ times as long as it was wide, but others say the ratio should be 4:3. You can investigate that, as well as the size of the kite. Grandpa also bowed the crossbar upward and held it taut with string, but he never explained why. Perhaps you can.

Once made, the frame can be laid on the paper. Cut the paper several inches wider than the frame. Fold the edges of the paper over the string onto the back of the paper and secure with glue or model airplane cement.

When you're ready to fly the kite, you may find that the point at which you fasten the line to the bridle has to be adjusted as well as the amount of tail. Much depends on the wind velocity. Some kite flyers use a bridle that attaches to all four corners of the kite.

After you've experimented with a conventional kite, you might like to try building a hexagonal kite, a box kite, and some other kites that you think will work well.

There's still much that is not known about kite flying. Perhaps you'll become an expert in this field and soar to new heights.

7
HEAT AND TEMPERATURE

Heat is a measure of the energy transferred from a warm body to a cooler one. When a body is warmed, its internal energy increases; that is, the kinetic energy of the molecules that make up the substance increases. The average kinetic energy of the molecules of a substance is directly proportional to the temperature of the substance.

Although technically heat is the energy transferred from a warm body to a cooler one, people often use the word *heat* to mean the thermal or internal energy of a body.

THE TEMPERATURE RANGE ON WINTER AND SUMMER DAYS

A maximum–minimum thermometer or a computer and thermometer interface will enable you to read the temperature range over a 24-h period. If you keep a record of the temperature range (the difference between maximum and minimum temperature) and the corresponding midrange temperature (average of maximum and minimum temperature) for each day through an entire winter, you will have the data you need to plot an interesting graph.

Use your data to plot the temperature range as a function of the midrange temperature. What pattern do you notice on your graph? At what average (midrange) temperature does the temperature range tend to be a minimum? Can you explain why?

If you collected data for an entire year, how do you think the temperature ranges for summer days would compare with those for winter days? Would it make a difference if you made your measurements near the ocean rather than inland?

WHY ANTIFREEZE?

In the winter, motorists mix a compound called ethylene glycol with water and use it as an antifreeze-coolant in automobile engines. Does the mixture, which is usually 50% glycol and 50% water, increase the coolant's specific heat?

To find out, put 100 g of cold water at about 10°C (50°F) in a Styrofoam cup supported by a glass or plastic beaker, as shown in Figure 17. (Why should the water be at a temperature below the temperature of the room?) **Put on safety glasses** and place an immersion heater, which you can buy at a supermarket, into the water. (Be sure the heater plug has three prongs and will be grounded when in use.) Plug the heater cord into a wall outlet for exactly 30 s. **Never plug in the immersion heater unless the heating coil is in a liquid.** After disconnecting the heater, stir the liquid and record its final temperature.

From the temperature change and mass of the water, how much heat, in calories or joules, does the heater provide in a 30-s period?

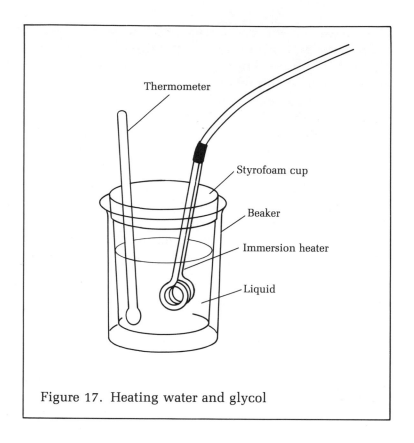

Thermometer

Styrofoam cup

Beaker

Immersion heater

Liquid

Figure 17. Heating water and glycol

Now that you know how much heat the heater delivers in 30 s, repeat the experiment using 100 g of glycol. From your data, what is the specific heat of the glycol? That is, how many calories or joules are required to change the temperature of 1 g of the liquid 1°C?

Most cars are sold with a 50–50 mixture of ethylene glycol and water in the cooling system. Make predictions about the density and specific heat of this mixture, then test your predictions. Were your predictions close to the values you measured?

The freezing point of water is 0°C; the freezing

point of glycol is $-17.9°C$. Predict the freezing point of the 50–50 mixture used as antifreeze, then try to find the freezing point. If you have difficulty measuring the freezing temperature in a freezer or in the cold winter air, ask a mechanic at a local garage. He or she will probably have this information.

Since, on the basis of specific heats, water is a better coolant than glycol, is there any reason, other than laziness, for keeping a glycol–water mixture in the cooling system all year?

One reason might be that the mixture boils at a temperature higher than that of water alone. Find out if this is the case by determining the boiling point of a 50–50 mixture of water and glycol. How does it compare with the boiling temperature of water?

Radiators are covered with a pressure cap so that the pressure within the system is higher than the pressure of the atmosphere outside. What is the reason for operating the cooling system under pressure?

ICE CREAM AND ENERGY

If you have an ice cream maker, you can measure the many energy transfers involved in making ice cream and have something good to eat when you finish your project. However, you'll have to use some of the ice cream to measure energy changes.

If you have an old-fashioned ice cream maker, you can determine the work you do in turning the crank to prepare the ice cream. If you have a newer model with an electric motor, you can determine the work done from the power rating, in watts, written on the machine and the time the machine operates.

What happens to the work done in turning the mixer?

To transform the rock salt and ice mixture from

32°F to −4°F (0°C to −20°C), how much heat must be transferred to the mixture?

To cool the ice cream mix from its original temperature to its freezing temperature requires a transfer of heat from the ice cream mix to the colder surrounding salt–ice mixture. You'll have to find the freezing point, the specific heat, and the heat of fusion (heat that must be transferred to freeze a gram) of the ice cream mix in order to make this calculation.

What will you need to know to determine the heat that must be transferred from the container to cool it from room temperature to the final temperature of the ice cream mix?

How does the heat transferred to the melting salt–ice mixture compare with the heat transferred from the ice cream mixture to make it freeze? Are any energy changes not accounted for?

EVAPORATION IS COOLING

On a hot day, how can you keep cool? A fan will help; so will an open window in a moving car. If you come out of a swimming pool and stand in a breeze, you may get so cold that you'll begin to shiver. Does this mean that moving air is cooler than still air? If you hold a thermometer in front of a fan, you will find that the temperature of the moving air is the same as that of the still air nearby. Try it for yourself! On the other hand, if you wrap a warm, wet cloth around a thermometer bulb and place it in front of a fan, the temperature will drop dramatically. It must be the evaporation of water that causes the temperature to fall.

Does the rate of evaporation affect cooling? To find out, pour equal volumes of hot water into three identical pans. Place the pans on newspapers several feet apart. Submerge a thermometer in each pan. To keep evaporation in one pan at a minimum, add enough cooking oil (a few drops should do) to cover the surface of the water. Let a fan blow air across the water in the second pan. Leave the third pan undisturbed in quiet air. Record the temperatures in each pan at 1-min intervals. After an hour or so, measure the water left in each pan. The volume of water lost divided by the time is the average rate of evaporation. How is the rate of evaporation related to the cooling rate of the water?

Design experiments of your own to see how temperature, humidity, the nature of the liquid, and the surface area of the liquid affect the rate of evaporation. You will need at least two setups for each experiment so that you can compare results. For example, if you were to investigate the effect of moving air on evaporation, you could place some water in front of a fan and an equal amount of water in another place where the air was still.

A BOOK FALLING
THROUGH ITS COVER
IS COOL

Find a heavy book with a book cover. Hold the book with your fingertips near the bottom of the cover. Place the book close to the floor and let the book slide quickly through its cover. Do this several times. Notice that the cover feels cooler after the book has slid through. But how can this be? Shouldn't friction produce heat? Are your senses fooling you, or are other factors involved that you haven't considered?

DOES ICE SUBLIMATE?

The change of a solid to a gas is called sublimation. The most common example is the change of dry ice (solid carbon dioxide) to its gaseous state. You may wonder whether ordinary ice changes to a gas without going through a liquid phase.

To find out, freeze some water in a glass, metal, or plastic tray. After it has frozen, cover parts of it with aluminum foil. If sublimation occurs, the aluminum foil should reduce the sublimation rate; consequently, after a few days, you should be able to see differences between the ice that is covered and the ice that is exposed.

Is there any evidence of sublimation after a day? After a week? After a month?

Can you design other ways to test for the sublimation of ice?

Do you think snow and crushed ice will sublimate? How do you think the rate of sublimation of snow and solid ice will compare? Design an experiment to test your prediction.

ICE UNDER PRESSURE

Water is one of the few substances that increase in volume (and, therefore, decrease in density) when frozen. Because a quantity of water has a smaller volume in the liquid state than in the solid state, applying a large pressure to ice will cause it to melt. It is the melting response of ice to pressure that enables you to skate on ice. The high pressure under a skate blade melts the ice and provides a thin, slippery film of water for you to glide through.

To see how variations in pressure affect the melting of ice, you can apply forces to thin wires that rest on an ice cube, as shown in Figure 18. **Ask an adult to help you cut slots in a thin board.** Use a pair of concrete blocks or some other objects to support the board. Then place ice cubes on the board with a loop of wire around them. By hanging a kilogram weight on

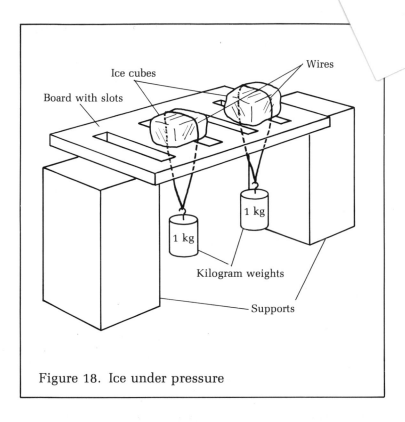

Figure 18. Ice under pressure

the lower end of the wire loop, you create a large pressure on the ice under the wire. Soon the wire will cut through the ice, but the ice above the wire will refreeze before the wire cuts all the way through the cube. This process is called *regelation*.

Do you think the diameter of the wire will affect the rate at which the wire passes through the ice? To find out, use identical ice cubes, but choose copper wires of different diameter. Under which wire is the pressure greatest?

Now try enameled and unenameled copper wire of the same diameter, or take two identical strands of enameled wire and melt the enamel off one of the wires. Does the insulation (enamel) on copper wires affect the rate of regelation?

Does the kind of material in the wire affect the rate at which the wire passes through the ice? What do you predict?

To test your prediction, gather a number of different uninsulated metal wires of the same diameter. If possible, find some nylon string with the same diameter as the wires. Test all of them on identical ice cubes using the same weight to pull each one through the ice. What do you find?

BUBBLELESS ICE CUBES

Look at an ice cube carefully. You'll see tiny air bubbles near the center of the cube. These bubbles were trapped inside the ice when it froze. The fact that some commercially made ice cubes contain no air bubbles is evidence that ice cubes can be made without air inside. But how? Try to design a method to make ice cubes that have no bubbles.

FOOTPRINTS IN THE FROST

Early on a clear, frosty morning, walk across a section of frosted grass where people seldom pass. When you return later in the day you will see that your footprints are still there. What color are they? How long do your footprints remain? Offer an hypothesis to explain how your footprints became etched on the grass. Then design an experiment to test your hypothesis.

WILL HOT WATER FREEZE
FASTER THAN COLD WATER?

Place equal volumes of hot and cold water in identical containers. Place the containers outside on a very cold winter day. Quite likely, the hot water will be frozen before the cold water. But how can this be? Can you offer an explanation for this odd behavior?

Many plumbers claim that hot water pipes will freeze before cold water pipes. Is there any truth to this claim? If so, how do you explain such a phenomenon?

EXPANSION AND TEMPERATURE

Look carefully at a bridge or the rails in a railroad track. There are spaces between the ends of the rails and bridge sections that allow the metal to expand without buckling when the temperature rises.

With a little care, you can measure the expansion of different metals and glass. Expansion is usually measured in units of length change per unit length per degree. Thus, if a 1-m length of metal expands 1.0 mm (0.001 m) for each degree change in temperature, its coefficient of expansion is 0.001 m/m°C, or 0.001/°C, since the units m/m cancel.

You'll need some metal and glass tubes about a meter (2 to 4 ft) long. Try to find tubes of different metals and glass with different diameters and thicknesses. Place one of the metal tubes on a board that rests near the edge of a table. Wrap a piece of tape around the tube close to one end. Clip a clothespin around the tape on the tube and fasten it in place with a C-clamp, as shown in Figure 19. Near the other end of the tube, slide a T-pin with a dial attached under the tube so that when the tube expands, the dial will turn. Use a rubber band and thumbtack to hold the tube firmly against the pin without preventing the tube from expanding.

Use flexible rubber tubing to connect the fixed end of the metal tube to a source of steam. A piece of tubing larger than a thermometer bulb and the metal

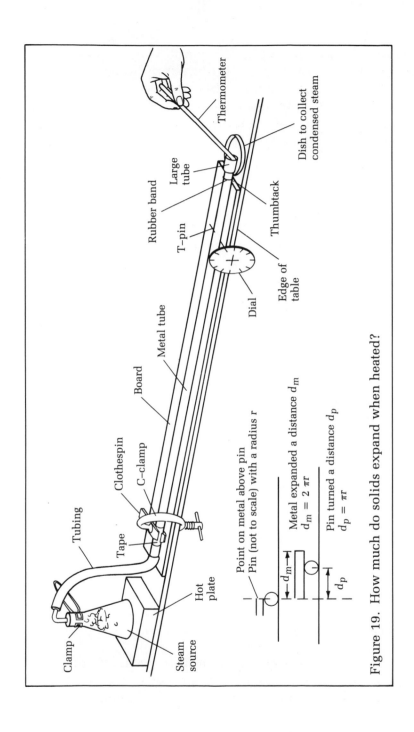

Figure 19. How much do solids expand when heated?

tube itself can be placed on the end of the tube that is free to move. Collect condensed steam in a saucer under the open end of the tube.

Measure the length of the tube between the C-clamp and the pin. Record the temperature of the room, and then heat the steam generator to force steam through the tube. When the tube stops expanding, record the angle through which the pin turned. Place a thermometer bulb in the large piece of tubing at the free end of the metal tube and measure the temperature of the steam. What was the temperature change of the metal tube that caused it to expand?

The change in length of the tube can be determined from the diameter of the pin and the angle through which it turned. However, as you can see from the drawing in Figure 19, the metal expands twice the distance that the pin turns because the pin rolls along the board; it does not turn in place.

Calculate the coefficient of expansion for various metals and glass. Is the coefficient related to the diameter of the tube? To its thickness? To the kind of metal or glass?

Design a method for finding the coefficient of expansion for liquids. If you decide to put your method to work, **ask for adult help. Don't heat flammable liquids!**

A BIMETALLIC THERMOSTAT

A thermostat is a switch that is turned on and off by changes in temperature. Contact is made and broken by means of a bimetallic strip made from two metals fastened firmly together. As the strip warms or cools, it bends because the two metals expand or contract different amounts for the same temperature change.

To make a simple bimetallic strip, cut and straighten a strip of thin steel 1 in (2.5 cm) wide and about 6 to

12 in (15 to 30 cm) long, from an ordinary tin can. Next, cut a strip of aluminum of equal length from an aluminum can. Fasten the two strips together by spreading epoxy glue along the surface of the strips. Put the two strips together against the glue and place them under a board with a heavy weight on it so that the two metals will become firmly stuck together.

Clamp one end of the bimetallic strip to the edge of a chair, stool, or table. Fix a sheet of cardboard or heavy paper beside the other end of the strip. Make a mark on the sheet to indicate the position of the free end of the strip. Now heat the bimetallic strip with a burning match or candle. Notice how the metal bends. Which metal expanded more, steel or aluminum?

Build other bimetallic strips using different metals. Which of the metals tested seems to lengthen the most when heated? Which combination bends the least? Which two metals would make the most sensitive thermostat?

8

SOLAR

ENERGY

Energy comes in various forms—kinetic, potential, thermal, and nuclear—but the one form of energy that costs us nothing is solar energy. As the world's supply of fossil fuels diminishes, the use of solar energy is likely to increase.

When people talk of solar energy, they usually think of sunlight falling on solar collectors or photovoltaic cells. But solar energy also produces wind, rain, hurricanes, and thunderstorms. Windmills utilize the kinetic energy in the wind, but winds acquire their energy from the sun.

BE A SCIENCE EDITOR

If you read textbooks, magazines, and newspaper articles carefully, you often will find errors. This is particularly true of writings related to solar energy. For example, here is one from a newspaper: "The energy output of these photovoltaic cells is 12 volts."

Here's another from an article on skin cancer:

"You should stay indoors at midday when the sun is directly overhead."

If you can detect the errors in these statements, you have a keen eye for detecting errors in scientific reporting. See how many errors you can detect as you read science-related books and articles. Keep copies of the errors you find together with your corrected versions. They could be the basis of an interesting project. You might want to write to editors, authors, and publishers, bringing to their attention the errors you have found.

A WINDOW BOX HEATER

Maybe you're not yet ready to design a solar home, but you can certainly construct a solar heater to help warm at least one room in a home or school. For a few dollars you can build a solar heater that will fit into a south window of a room, as shown in Figure 20.

First, build the outer shell, the upper end of which must be connected to the frame of a south window. To increase its heating capacity, you can make the solar absorbing surface of the heater wider than the window. Use 1- x 10-in boards for the sides and 3/8-in exterior plywood for the bottom.

Next, build an inner shell from 3/8-in plywood. Insulation, at least 3 1/2 in thick, should lie between the sides and bottom of the two shells. Spacers made from scrap wood can be used to hold the shells at proper separation.

A sheet of 3/8-in interior plywood will divide the inner shell into top and bottom sections. Leave a 4-in gap across the bottom of the inner box so that cool air descending under the divider can flow through the gap to the upper side of the divider and ascend back into the room as it warms. Use furring strips to support the divider about 2 in below the top of the inner

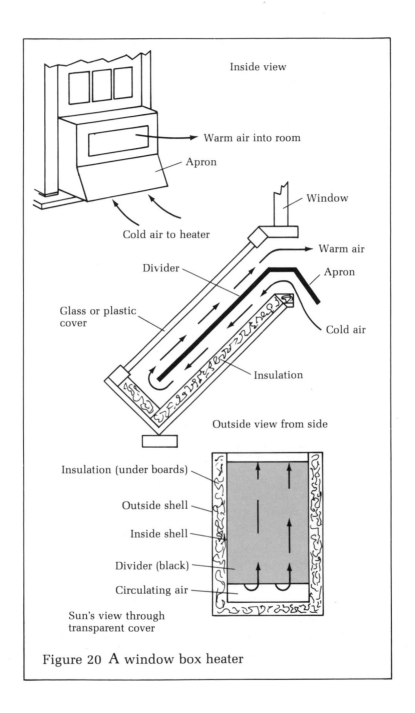

Inside view

Warm air into room

Apron

Cold air to heater

Window

Warm air

Divider

Apron

Glass or plastic cover

Cold air

Insulation

Outside view from side

Insulation (under boards)

Outside shell

Inside shell

Divider (black)

Circulating air

Sun's view through transparent cover

Figure 20 A window box heater

shell. Nail, staple, or glue the divider in place and apply a coat of flat black paint to it.

Build a connecting "tunnel" between the box and the window using 1 x 10-in boards. It too should have a divider with an apron where it enters the room (see drawing) so that cool air near the floor enters the lower side of the heater while warm air flows into the room from above the divider.

Use 1-in pine boards to cover the insulation between the shells. Lay a sheet of clear plastic (Sun-Lite is good) over the opening to enclose the air and allow solar energy to reach the black collecting surface. Nail or staple wood strips around the clear sheet to hold it firmly against the pine boards. Alternatively, an old storm window could be used in place of the clear plastic.

Finally, after you are sure the heater fits snugly into the window, the heater should be caulked, weather-stripped, and painted to prevent air leaks and to protect it from snow and rain.

How much does a heater like this reduce your family's heating bill?

SUNLIGHT TO ELECTRICITY

Solar energy is most commonly converted to heat, but it can also be changed into electricity and mechanical energy. You've probably seen solar calculators, which are powered by ordinary desk lamps. This is one example of how the ability to convert light to electricity is used commercially.

To see how electricity can be produced from sunlight, place a photovoltaic cell in a sunny place. Use wires to connect the cell to a sensitive ammeter or voltmeter. What evidence do you have that sunlight is producing electricity?

What happens if you shade the surface of the cell with your hand? What happens if you vary the angle between the sun's rays and the surface of the photovoltaic cell?

How could you use a small resistor and a sensitive voltmeter or ammeter to measure the power produced by the photovoltaic cell? (Remember, $P = V^2/R$ or $P = I^2R$.)

What happens to the power developed if you connect photovoltaic cells in series or parallel?

Can you design and build a photovoltaic battery that could be used to produce enough electricity to meet the power needs of a small building? Bear in mind you must find some way to store the electrical energy unless its use is to be limited to sunny daylight hours.

A PHOTOELECTROCHEMICAL CELL*

Imagine a photoelectric cell that would work in the dark. Impossible you might think. But suppose part of the energy produced by a photoelectric cell is used to charge an electrochemical cell. After sunset, when the photoelectric cell stops working, the charged chemical cell could then be used to provide electricity.

In the November 12, 1987, issue of *Nature*, you will find an article describing just such a photoelectrochemical cell. It was developed by Stuart Licht at the Weizmann Institute in Israel.

See if you can devise a similar, but more efficient, cell. The production of such cells at reasonable prices could have a profound effect on the way electricity is produced. In reasonably sunny parts of the world, each building might have its roof covered with photoelectrochemical cells that would provide all the electricity required for that building.

USING THE SUN TO DISTILL WATER

In arid lands water may be worth more than oil. In some of these places there is plenty of water—oceans of it—but it is salt water. When drunk, salt water only increases thirst, and most plants cannot tolerate it. However, by the process of distillation, salt can be separated from water.

Unfortunately, the distillation of seawater requires energy, which is expensive. But often, arid lands are sunny, and solar energy is free. Consequently, some countries, at considerable cost, are beginning to use sunlight to obtain potable water from the abundant seawater that is nearby.

As a start, you can make a model solar device for distilling salt water. You'll need two large aluminum pans. One of the pans can serve as a control in the experiments you'll conduct. Paint the inside of both pans with flat black paint and let it dry. Place one end of each pan on a block. At the lower end of each pan cut about ½ in (1 cm), from top toward bottom, along the corners of the pan, as shown in Figure 21. Fold the flap you have made down along the inside of the pan. The opening you have made will allow water to flow downward along a glass cover placed on the pan. The water will drip into a collecting pan placed below the end of the glass plate.

Place both pans in sunlight. If they are identical, you should get about equal amounts of distilled water in the same amount of time. Once you are satisfied that the two pans are very nearly the same, you can begin experimenting. For example, do you get better results if the sides of the experimental pan are covered with an insulating material such as newspaper or Styrofoam? Does it make a difference if you add black ink or food coloring to the water? Do you get a greater rate of production if the pan is covered with plastic or

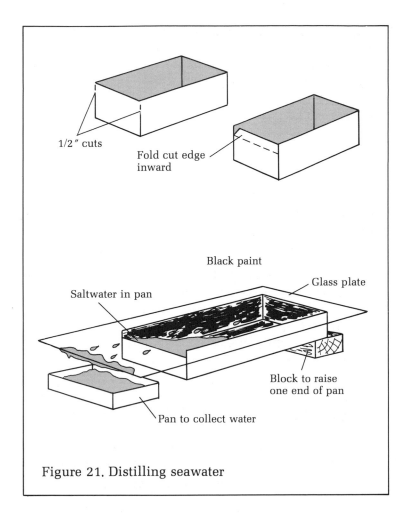

1/2 ″ cuts

Fold cut edge inward

Black paint

Glass plate

Saltwater in pan

Block to raise one end of pan

Pan to collect water

Figure 21. Distilling seawater

plastic wrap instead of glass? Will two panes of glass with an air space between them increase the rate at which distilled water is produced? Does the type or color of paint have any effect?

Having experimented with this model, design a large-scale means of producing potable water for a home or for a town or city.

Perhaps you can develop other methods for providing water for arid areas. In some places, such as Bermuda, rain that falls on roofs is captured and stored in cisterns. Several countries are considering the possibility of towing large icebergs from the Antarctic. The meltwater from the icebergs could then be used as a freshwater source. Would this method work? Does freezing as well as boiling eliminate salt from seawater?

SOLAR ENERGY MACHINES

If the energy in sunlight can be used to distill water and to generate electricity, it should be possible to design solar machines. One such machine is shown in Figure 22. You can build a similar one for yourself. It uses an airstream created by solar energy to turn a pinwheel. To avoid effects due to random air currents, the machine should be surrounded by cardboard.

How is the pinwheel's spin rate affected by clouds? By the time of day? By different colored light? By the color of the can? By other light sources? By other effects?

Build other machines of your own design that are powered by the sun. Can any of them be developed into practical machines for commercial use?

WINDMILLS

When sunlight falls on the atmosphere, the air is usually heated unevenly. This gives rise to convection currents on a global scale that we call winds. The kinetic energy of wind, which has its origin in solar energy, can be used to do useful work. Sailing ships were one of humankind's first use of wind power. It was the development of windmills that enabled the

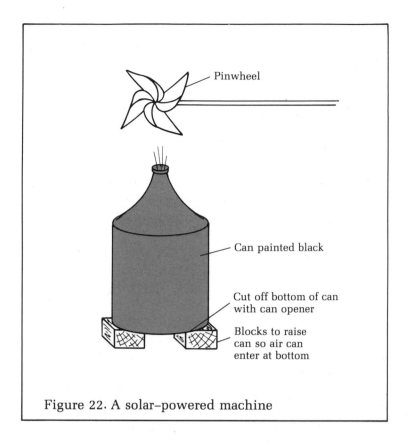

Figure 22. A solar–powered machine

Netherlands to become a leading industrial nation in the 17th century.

Today, wind power plays a small role as an energy source, but as the supply of fossil fuels dwindles during the next century, wind may once again become a major source of energy.

As with direct solar energy, the energy in wind is not always a reliable source. It's true that the wind may blow at night as well as in the daytime, but in many places there may be days when there is little or no wind at all. Consequently, some way has to be found to store the energy available from the wind when it does blow. In many places this is done by using a windmill to turn an electric generator that charges batteries.

Here are several projects related to windmills:

Building a Model Windmill
To see how a windmill converts wind into kinetic energy and then into electricity, you can build and operate a model windmill.

To begin, cut a square 1¼ in (3 cm) on a side from a piece of balsa wood ½ in (13 mm) thick. Use a fine hacksaw blade to make diagonal grooves on opposite sides of the block, as shown in Figure 23A. Note that the angles of the grooves are the reverse of one another.

Use a ruler to find the exact center of the face on one side of the block. With a nail or a small hand drill, make a small hole about ¼ in (6 mm) deep. The hole should be slightly narrower than the diameter of the shaft of a 1.5-volt toy D.C. motor on which the block will be mounted.

Before placing the block on the motor shaft, cut a tongue depressor in half. Put a little glue into each of the grooves you cut in the wood block. Slide one tongue depressor half into each groove. While the glue is drying, connect the wire leads from the motor to a 100-Ω resistor. Then connect a voltmeter (0 to 6 V) to the resistor so that it is wired in parallel with the motor, as shown in Figure 23B.

Once the glue has dried, mount the propeller block on the motor shaft (it should fit snugly) and place the propeller in front of a turning fan. If the voltmeter needle moves the wrong way, reverse its wire leads. What happens to the voltmeter readings as the wind speed is varied? What happens to the power developed? You can find the power from the equation $P = V^2/R$. For example, if the voltmeter reads 2.0 V, the power can be calculated as

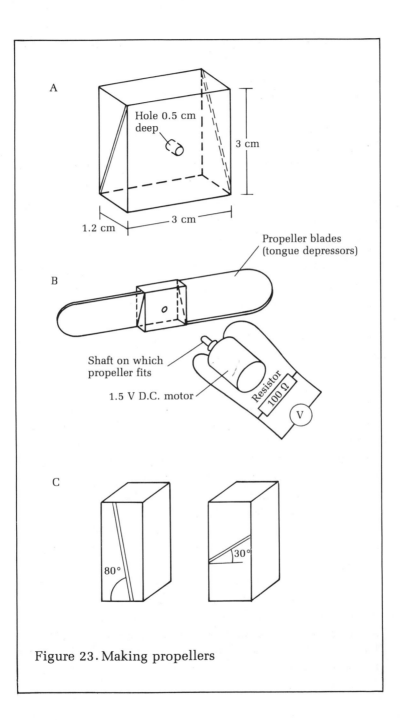

A

Hole 0.5 cm deep

3 cm

3 cm

1.2 cm

Propeller blades
(tongue depressors)

B

Shaft on which
propeller fits

1.5 V D.C. motor

Resistor 100 Ω

V

C

80°

30°

Figure 23. Making propellers

$$P = V^2/R = (2.0\ V)^2/100\Omega = 0.04\ W$$

Show that the unit volts squared divided by ohms gives watts as the unit of power.

You can vary the angle of the propeller blades by cutting the grooves at different angles, as shown in Figure 23C. Use a protractor to set the angles. Is one angle more effective than another in producing electric power at a given wind speed? If you see a trend, perhaps you can enhance the power production by changing the angle still more.

Can you generate enough electrical energy to light a flashlight bulb?

How does wind speed affect the power generated? To measure wind speed, you can build a meter like the one shown in Figure 24. The meter can be calibrated by holding it out the window of a car moving at known speeds through still air. **Be careful! Do this in an area where there is no traffic.**

Propeller Size

Will a propeller twice as large provide twice as much power? To find out, cut a balsa wood block and make grooves at the angle that you found produces maximum power. Then take two tongue depressors and simply square off one end to make it straight. Mount one entire depressor in each slot to create a propeller that is just about twice as big.

What other variables must you control in order to find the effect of propeller size on the development of electric power?

Another way to make a propeller that has twice the blade area is to cut grooves in the other two sides of the wood block so that you have a four-bladed prop. Is the power developed by this propellor the same as that for a double-size two-blade prop with the same propeller angle and wind speed?

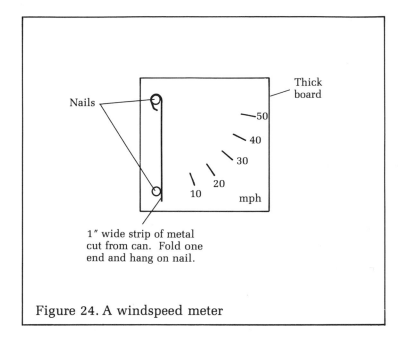

Figure 24. A windspeed meter

In terms of power developed, do you find the same effects when you change the wind speed using a four-blade prop that you found with a two-blade prop?

A Better Propeller
Investigate the various types of windmill props such as Helix Rotors, Savonius Rotors, and conventional props that you may encounter in your research. Make small-scale models of these various props and test them. Then see if you can develop a propeller of your own design.

A Better Windmill
Now that you have investigated a variety of windmill propellers, you might like to try building an actual windmill that can do some useful work. What kind of propeller will you use? What is the best site for your

windmill? How will you store some of the energy produced? Can you build a windmill that can be used commercially?

ENERGY FROM BIOMASS*

Another indirect source of solar energy is the decomposition of organic matter. This matter is produced as a result of photosynthesis, in which sunlight, together with carbon dioxide and water, is converted into food. Eventually the food is incorporated into plant tissue. As you may know, it is possible to produce flammable gases and liquids by heating wood and other kinds of plant tissue.

Wood, sugar beet, corn, and various grains can be converted to alcohol fuels. In fact, gasohol, a mixture of gasoline and alcohol, is sold as a fuel for use in automobiles.

A question that many people ask is whether it is economically feasible to use a fuel to decompose organic matter into another fuel. For example, burning natural gas to decompose wood into methyl alcohol may cost more than the value of the alcohol produced. However, if solar energy or bacteria could be used to decompose organic matter into useful fuels, the process would make sense economically.

See if you can develop an inexpensive method of producing fuel from waste organic matter.* **Be sure to work closely with a knowledgeable adult on this project. The materials you will be producing are flammable liquids or gases.**

SCIENCE SUPPLY COMPANIES

Carolina Biological
Supply Co.
2700 York Road
Burlington, NC 27215

Central Scientific Co.
(CENCO)
11222 Melrose Avenue
Franklin Park, IL 60131

Connecticut Valley Bio-
logical Supply Co., Inc.
82 Valley Road
Southampton, MA 01073

Damon/Instructional
Systems Div.
80 Wilson Way
Westwood, MA 02090

Delta Education
P.O. Box M
Nashua, NH 03061

Edmund Scientific Co.
101 East Gloucester Pike
Barrington, NJ 08007

Fisher Scientific Co.
4901 West LeMoyne St.
Chicago, IL 60651

Frey Scientific Co.
905 Hickory Lane
Mansfield, OH 44905

McKilligan Supply Corp.
435 Main Street
Johnson City, NY 13790

Nasco Science
901 Janesville Road
Fort Atkinson, WI 53538

Nasco West Inc.
P.O. Box 3837
Modesto, CA 95352

Prentice-Hall Allyn &
Bacon
Equipment Division
10 Oriskany Drive
Tonawanda, NY 14150-
6781

Schoolmasters Science
P.O. Box 1941
Ann Arbor, MI 48106

Ward's Natural Science
Establishment, Inc.
5100 West Henrietta
Road
P.O. Box 92912
Rochester, NY 14692

FURTHER READING

INTRODUCTION

Beller, Joel. *So You Want to Do a Science Project.* New York: Arco, 1982.

Loiry, William S. *Winning with Science.* Sarasota, Fla. Loiry Publishing, 1983.

Tocci, Salvatore. *How to Do a Science Fair Project.* New York: Watts, 1986.

Van Deman, Barry A., and MacDonald, Ed. *Nuts & Bolts: A Matter of Fact Guide to Science Projects.* Harwood Heights, Ill.: The Science Man Press, 1980.

CHAPTER 1

Apfel, Necia H. *Astronomy and Planetology: Projects for Young Scientists.* New York: Watts, 1983.

Asimov, Isaac. *How Did We Find Out About the Speed of Light?* New York: Walker, 1986.

Dexter, W.A. *A Field Guide to Astronomy without a Telescope.* Boston: Houghton Mifflin, 1971.

Gallant, Roy A. *The Planets: Exploring the Solar System.* New York: Macmillan, 1982.

Gardner, Robert. *Ideas for Science Projects.* New York: Watts, 1986.

Greenleaf, Peter. *Experiments in Space Science.* New York: Arco, 1981.

Heuer, Kenneth. *Rainbows, Halos, & Other Wonders: Light & Color in the Atmosphere.* New York: Dodd, Mead, 1978.

Haber-Schaim, Uri; Dodge, John; and Walter, James. *PSSC Physics.* Lexington, Mass.: Heath, 1985.

Kaufmann, William J. III. *Universe.* New York: Freeman, 1985.

MacRobert, Alan M. *Backyard Astronomy.* Ringwood, N.J.: Sky Publishing, 1986.

McKay, David W, and Smith, Bruce G. *Space Science Projects for Young Scientists.* New York: Watts, 1986.

CHAPTER 2

Aylesworth, Thomas G. *Storm Alert: Understanding Weather Disasters.* New York: Messner, 1980.

Battan, Louis J. *Weather.* Englewood Cliffs, N.J.: Prentice-Hall, 1985.

_____. *Weather in Your Life.* New York: Freeman, 1985.

Boys, Charles V. *Soap Bubbles.* New York: Dover, 1959.

Boy Scouts of America. *Geology.* Irving, Tex.: BSA, 1985.

Bubbles & Bubble Blowers. San Diego: Green Tiger Press, 1982.

Braker, William P., and Fisher, Ed L. *Marine Aquariums,* Neptune, N.J. TFH Publications, 1984.

Challand, Helen J. *Activities in the Earth Sciences.* Chicago: Children's Press, 1982.

Gardner, Robert. *Water: The Life-Sustaining Resource.* New York: Messner, 1983.

Gunston, Bill. *Water.* Lexington, Mass.: Silver Burdett, 1982.

Hessler, Edward W. *Acid Rain Science Projects.* St. Paul, Minn.: Acid Rain Foundation, 1987.

Paysan, Klaus. *Aquarium Fish from Around the World.* Minneapolis, Minn.: Lerner Publications, 1970.

Whitlock, Ralph. *Water Divining & Other Dowsing: A Practical Guide.* North Pomfret, Vt.: David & Charles, 1982.

Zubrowski, Bernie. *Bubbles: A Children's Museum Activity Book:* Boston: Little, Brown, 1979.

CHAPTER 3

Dunbar, Robert E. *The Heart and Circulatory System: Projects for Young Scientists.* New York: Watts, 1984.

Storrs, Graham. *Understanding the Senses.* Lexington, Mass.: Silver Burdett, 1985.

CHAPTER 4

Castleman, Michael. *Cold Cures.* New York: Fawcett, 1987.

Ellis, Richard. *The Book of Whales.* New York: Knopf, 1985.

Ford, Norman. *Eighteen Natural Ways to Beat the Common Cold.* New Canaan, Conn.: Keats, 1987.

Gardner, Robert. *The Whale Watchers' Guide.* New York: Messner, 1984.

Gardner, Robert, and Webster, David. *Science in Your Backyard.* New York: Messner, 1987.

Harrison, H.H. *A Field Guide to Bird's Nests.* Boston: Houghton Mifflin, 1975.

Jacobson, Morris K., and Franz, David R. *Wonders of Snails and Slugs.* New York: Dodd, Mead, 1986.

Lilly, John C. *Communication Between Man and Dolphin: The Possibilities of Talking with Other Species.* New York: Crown, 1987.

Miller, Robyn. *Robyn's Book: A True Diary.* New York: Scholastic, 1986.

Norris, Kenneth S. *Whales, Dolphins, and Porpoises.* Berkeley and Los Angeles: University of California Press, 1978.

Payne, Roger. *Communication and Behavior of Whales.* Boulder, Colo.: Westview, 1983.

Peterson, Roger T. *Birds Over America.* New York: Dodd, 1983.

Smith, Norman F. *How Fast Do Your Oysters Grow?* New York: Messner, 1982.

Stokes, Donald W. *A Guide to the Behavior of Common Birds.* Boston: Little, Brown, 1983.

Woodsen, Meg. *I'll Get to Heaven Before You Do!* Nashville, Tenn.: Abingdon, 1985.

CHAPTER 5

Beller, Joel. *Experimenting with Plants.* New York: Arco, 1985.

Gardner, Robert, and Webster, David. *Science in Your Backyard.* New York: Messner, 1987.

Research Problems in Biology Investigations for Students. 3 vols. New York: Oxford University Press, 1976.

CHAPTER 6

Barry, James D. *Ball Lightning and Bead Lightning: Extreme Forms of Atmospheric Activities.* New York: Plenum, 1980.

Rutherford, F. James; Holton, Gerald; and Watson, Fletcher G. *Project Physics.* New York: Holt, 1975.

_____. *The Project Physics Course Handbook.* New York: Holt, 1975.

CHAPTER 7

Gardner, Robert. *Energy Projects for Young Scientists.* New York: Watts, 1987.
_____. *Save That Energy.* New York: Messner, 1981.
Haber-Schaim, Uri. *Energy: A Sequel to IPS.* Englewood Cliffs, N.J.: Prentice-Hall, 1983.
Oei, Paul D.; Sorenson, Eugene W.; and Chang, Chih-Ming. *Projects and Experiments in Energy.* New York: National Energy Foundation, 1982.

CHAPTER 8

Alternative Energy Handbook: Emmaus, Pa.: Rodale Press, 1979.
Anderson, Bruce, with Riordan, Michael. *The Solar Home Book.* Harrisville, N.H.: Brick House, 1976.
Gardner, Robert. *Energy Projects for Young Scientists.* New York: Watts, 1987.
_____. *Save That Energy.* New York: Messner, 1981.
Gipe, Paul. *Wind Energy: How to Use It.* Harrisburg, Pa.: Stackpole, 1983.
Haber-Schaim, Uri, *Energy: A Sequel to IPS.* Englewood Cliffs, N.J.: Prentice-Hall, 1983.
Keyes, John. *Harnessing the Sun to Heat Your Home.* Dobbs Ferry, N.Y.: Morgan & Morgan, 1974.
Oei, Paul D.; Sorenson, Eugene W.; and Chang, Chih-Ming. *Projects and Experiments in Energy.* New York: National Energy Foundation, 1982.
Wolfe, Ralph, and Clegg, Peter. *Home Energy for the Eighties.* Charlotte, Vt.: Garden Way Publishing, 1979.

INDEX